Common Good

Bahaa Jameel

authorHOUSE®

AuthorHouse™ UK Ltd.
500 Avebury Boulevard
Central Milton Keynes, MK9 2BE
www.authorhouse.co.uk
Phone: 08001974150

First published by AuthorHouse 06/23/2011

ISBN: 978-1-4567-8284-9 (sc)
ISBN: 978-1-4567-8285-6 (e)

Introduction

In the third world countries the governments that reach to the power by military coup, in their attempting to dominate their people, use many destroying policies that impact badly and directly their nations and citizens and indirectly drive their nations toward underdevelopment.

Public interest is one of the forms that used in my country to deprive thousands of civil service employees from their jobs, starve them, make them homeless and substitute them with people who are blind obedient and loyal to the regime without giving any consideration to the competence. They do this in order to have strict control over all important and vital state facilities and instituations.

In cases of presence of similar governments we would have nothing to do except keep writing to make the free people around the world aware of the bitter inequity imposed on the human beings and humanity in those countries and make our experiences available to the benefit of all peoples.

BAHAA. JAMEEL

(1)

The sound of the bell of the morning queue at Madame Asma's Secondary School for the girls rang loudly and Karbous ringing it violently as he used to do since twenty years ago, not a minute earlier, not a minute later.

The iron rod suspended on the branch of the old Neem tree between the headmaster office and the outer wall of the school oscillated vehemently and remained oscillating even after the bald, thin, vein-handed and curve backed man had put down the iron handle in its usual place and stepped lightly towards the main gate. The girls scattered in the school courtyards and classes hastened towards the morning queue square when they heard the strong familiar sound echoing in their ears.

The girls who arrived late hurried towards the blue outer gate in the middle of the long faint yellow wall before it is closed and expose them to punishment. In doing so, they stirred a wave of dust and which frightened a flock of goats which try to catch up some falling leaves moved by the gentle breeze from time to time.

The necks of the workers of the fuel station which is separated by only few meters from the blue gate stretched curiously and cheerfully ignoring the shouts of the lorry driver urging them to quickly fill up his tank with fuel, and the eyes of the staff of the police center which lies at the southern end of the school wall widened and circulated in their cavities while their lines were disrupted in front of the tall well – build lieutenant who stood erect before them as if he is a flag – staff . He was compelled to shout at them angrily with his sonorous voice which reached the female staff of the Social Welfare home who laughed

1

delightedly exchanging mockery at his shout which they are used to hear at this time every day. And the movement of the worker of dar alssalam kafteria which lies at the eastern end of the school wall has increased going to and fro which they pretend of collecting empty tea cups left by some employees of the locality and farm workers after drinking their morning tea. The whole place was full with movement.

Inside the school Ustaz Jalal stood in the middle of the spaces courtyard which face the entrance from the western side and the grand courtyard from the eastern side which the students going towards the queue square following at the same time the last girl to enter the school to make sure that the entrance was closed in the fixed time when he saw a girl walking slowly although he was standing watching and although she was the last one to enter the school. She appeared, in the midst of this tripping movement as she is a sad misplaced pointing or a funeral song in a wedding ceremony, he looked scrutinizing at her beautiful face which was covered with a cloud of sadness. He knew she is Salma. He kept following her with his look while she was carrying her bag loosely until it was about to touch the ground.

He was absorbed in his thought and remembered that this is the second time this week to see this girl so sad and disheartened, the first time was on Saturday when he was passing in front of her class, he saw her from the window sitting alone, putting her school bag on the old wooden table in front of her after all her class mates went out holding her scarf with both hands drying the tears which wetted her cheeks. He stood looking at her asking himself why she was crying. He thought that she was weeping for something related to school. He entered the class, she felt he was entering and hastened to wipe off the tears, sitting straight; covering her head again, taking a big book from her bag and sinking her face in it, Some of her sadness crept to his heart and crouched on his chest while he was greeting her. She exchanged his greeting in a low smothered voice, He asked her why she was alone and why didn't she leave the class to take her breakfast as other girls, She told him that she has an assignment to do, that her breakfast is in her bag and that she will take it after doing her assignment, He asked whether there is anything annoying her. She said no. He was forced to ask her why was she crying, She was confused but replied quickly "perhaps it is allergy that make my eye full of tears from time to time ", in fact she has no assignment and there isn't any breakfast in her bag, it is true that allergy makes her eyes full of tears sometimes put not this time, Ustaz JALAL realized that and realized that she is in trouble. He also knew that she wasn't tell him anything now, he was in his way to see the doctor, that famous doctor whom Ustaz JALAL had waited for three month to obtain an appointment to meet him today, he has just enough time to reach the doctors clinic . To miss that appointment means that he had to wait for a further three months at least to obtain a new appointment but in spite of all that he went back towards the teachers office ignoring his acute headache, the pressing strain he was feeling and the important appointment with the doctor, he passed on his way near the flower basin lying in the middle of the spacious courtyard surrounded by the school classes and saw a red rose trodden by feet stuck in the clay below it, He bowed anxiously, held the stem yearningly and drew it tenderly from the clay, he was afraid that the stem might have broken but he found it safe and sound, He took his handkerchief and rubbed the stem carefully to clean it, then took the rose sprinkled some water in it, and left it . The rose shrub stood erects again and stirred gracefully right and left by the action of the air as if thanking him. He smiled contently, although there are some plankton still stuck in the small red leaves he continue his way truthfully that it's knew well how to thrown- it a way after it stood up again. He reached the office of the Arabic and mathematics department, knocked the open door and heard a female voice inviting him to come in, He took one step inward in a way that he shall see and be seen by those in the office, First he saw Hafsa, the Arabic language teacher, and Salma's class tutor sitting at her large office supporting the telephone receiver to her ear with her left shoulder turning a precious golden pen between her fingers . Her yellow scarf and sleeves of her green blouse cold be seen clearly behind her white transparent dress. Along earring at the end which was a large round red disc was hanging down her ears, she was as usual, busy in a whispering conversation which cannot be heard by the nearest person to her . She seemed as if she were a circus player in an interval. On her left Iqpal, the school social supervisor, assigned with the task of solving the students' problems was sitting turning the pages of an illustrated women magazine; she was wearing a fine white dress and a scarf around her round beautiful face. The scarf was completely matching with her soft complexion reflecting her fine taste in selecting her dresses. Hafsa wrinkled her eye brows annoyed when she saw him and her whispering got more lower experiencing that dual feeling which always occur to her whenever she meets with Ustaz Jalal and Iqbal in one place, Iqbal also had the same feeling whenever she sees Ustaz Jala, So she opened one of the drawers of her office stealthily and dropped the magazine quietly inside it. Samia, the teacher of mathematics who share the office with Hafsa and Iqpal didn't raise her head from the heap of exercise books dumped in front of her on the table until she heard him saying "Salmu alikum " and replied at the same time with Iqbal "Alaikum Alssalam "

He addressed Samia turning his eyes between Hafsa and Iqpal saying:

- It seems you have a lot of work as usual.
  She replied smiling:
- The endless mathematic exercises and questions as you know.
- Could you please see me at my office when you finish your work?
- If the matter is important, I will postpone the correction for another time, any way there is only half an hour for the end of the interval. After that I shall be busy to the end of the day, I have five lectures left.
  Ustaz JALAL replied seriously:
- The matter is quit important.
- In this case, I will join you after a little while.

Iqbal was following up the short dialogue between Ustaz JALAL and Ustaza Samia in anger and rage, but despite the numerous problems which broke out between Ustaz Jalal and herself since she received her work in this school and despite the fact that he was the only person who criticized her continuously for a long time and accused her by negligence and omission but some kind of jealousy always comes across her heart whenever she sees him talking to one of her female colleagues or asking about her . A Sort of jealousy that she has not explanation or justification known to her, at first, she always tried to deny it and attribute it not for its real cause, and this jealousy multiplies especially when she sees him speaking to Samia. she often sees him talking to her or coming to the office to assign some work to her or ask her to drop at his office, She often hear him praising her efforts and sincerity to her work and she hated her although Samia never mistreated or differed with her in anything .

IQBAL used to draw a false mask of irritation and displeasure on her face once she sees Ustaz JALAL to conceal her care about him,and hide her disturbance and yearning combined with her incessant feeling of jealousy, and she was able to deceive all those around her with that mask until they thought that she dislikes him and never bear to see him,but Hafsa felt her vexation in the tune of her voice, and noticed her concern about him in the features of her countenance she also observed her longing for him on her looks and loss of concentration. She is the only one who was not deceived by that mask because she knows her very well. Although Hafsa's detest of Ustaz JALAL is real and springs from her inner self and although she hates to meet him in any place, but meeting him with IQBAL in one place generates in her a dual and overlapping feeling, it is true that she hates his presence but she likes the effect left by that presence in IQBAL. The relationship between her irritation with his presence and the changes effected by that presence in the soul of her collogue is sheer reflex relationship, the more the vexation irritation and disturbance of IQBAL increases, the lesser gets her indignation about his presence until she finally forgets him completely and all her thoughts become focused on the vast change that occurs to IQBAL and the comfort which creeps to her soul as though a gentle breeze infiltrates' through a tiny vent in a dark room tightly closed, particularly when she sees those wide confident eyes lose their confidence and their looks change to hesitant and perplexed looks when she sees that pretty face covered with a cloud of pain, when she sees those compact radiant lips tremble nervously and when she sees those fine thin fingers move restlessly . Although she was preoccupied in her telephone conversation when Ustaz JALAL entered the office, but she did her best not to miss anything going on in the office and at the same time not to interrupt her whispering conversation, she soon felt that her inner self stated to pick that comfortable sensation while watching her colleagues face eagerly., when Ustaz JALAL went out followed by Smia, and IQBAL stretched her lips, opened and shut her table drawer several times without taking anything from it and muttered some words in suppressed indignation, her smile got wider revealing her yellowish-block teeth, and her feeling of comfort reached its climax . She continued her conversation her face surfeited with pleasure and elation as if she has just received the news of her betrothal to the knight of her dreams.

Ustaz JALAL put aside the aspirin tablets and took a sip of tea from the tea - cup on the table in front of him then said to Samia who sat on the chair opposite to his office:

- There is a student who seems to be suffering a problem; it seems that her problem is rather serious... She studies in the third class. As usual I need your help to know her problem to assist her to overcome it.
- Perhaps you are referring to Salma?
  He said while a faint a smile has been drawing on his lips
- How did you know I am referring to Salma??
- Have you forgotten that I teach her class mathematics and see her every day??
- Since when did you know that she has a problem??
- "Several weeks ago "
- Why didn't you tell me as long as you know so that we might work together to solve the problem.
- You are so busy during the last period more over I know that your health is not quite well, so I preferred not to increase your troubles, I have studied her file carefully but I didn't succeed in persuading her to tell me what she is suffering from. certainly I would tell you once I discover something definite "

He took a long breath and said "tell me immediately all that you know about her".

Samia sighed and sat straight saying"

- Salma came to school from the intermediate stage with excellent marks .Her file shows that she was the top of her class since the first primary form until the end of the basic stage and her admission to Madame Asma's school, but at end of her first year here, she obtained an ordinary result which did not conform with her previous record at though she did not seem to experience a problem or complain from something .During her second year she was transferred to the social instructor twice, she became more isolated and introvert and her result worsened . This year she joined my class, when I noticed that she is always absent – minded and sad, I was convinced that she is facing a difficult problem. I tried, in my own way, to know what is wrong with her but up to know I didn't succeed. I sent to her father to discuss the matter with him but unfortunately he did not come.

Ustaz Jalal pressed his forehead strongly to alleviate the horrible pain he is feeling and said:

- "Since when did you send for him?

- Last week. I gave Salma a message to deliver to him but until now he didn't come to see me "

- The fact that he didn't come indicates that the problem is not easy. Please go on your attempts with her I will try to know why he didn't come, I will do my best to meet him today or tomorrow at most. What you have mentioned is so important. We shouldn't wait more than this. The future of a brilliant girl is threatened. Any day that will pass in this year cannot be compensated easily. Our duty dictates on us that we must save the future of this girl.

Ustaz JALAL was suddenly aware that the girls had aligned and the teachers in charge of the morning queue are waiting for him. He harried towards the square firmly determined to see Salma's father …. Sees him today whatever it might cost him.

[2]

Hafsa, IQBAL and another teacher were appointed in Madame Asma's School a year and a half before the date Ustaz JALAL knew about Selma's problem. Although Hafsa and IQBAL were companions in and outside the school, yet, they are contradictory in everything, IQBAL is the daughter of a rich and influential man in the ruling party which took power through a military coup led by a partisan officer several years ago aborting a democratic government propping its way during the first years to power . Hafsa is the daughter of a simple farmer at a remote village in her poor rural areas. IQBAL has brown complexion, graceful body, soft hair, wide eyes, extraordinary beauty and excessive femininity... Hafsa was whit – complexioned, tall board- shouldered, narrow – eyed, and black spots spread on her cheeks, forehead and big nose save for her small eyes and thin lips. IQBAL was content, and inclined to comfortable, lazy and luxury life while Hafsa was active, vital, ambitious, and has astringe greed for money, power and fame. They met for the first time at the university in a lecture hall. Since Hafsa was always eager to befriend the girl of which family since she is thirsty, body and soul, to keep close to those whose life is full of luxury and since she heard a lot about IQBAL s father and his great influence in the ruling party when she was a member of a women organization in her remote area before she come to study at the university, she decided to strengthen her relationship with IQBAL and she did her best to get closer to her and be her friend. She knew that if she was able to get closer to IQBAL father, she will gain his support which she knew will need in the future. Although Hafsa has first joined the ruling party out of her conviction with the principles of justice, equality, and right of decent life

9

like most poor and marginalized people who are usually quicker than other people to believe in the slogans of virtuous values, but she was soon affected with those around her and the environment in which she started her political activity. Personal gain, acquisition of money, and occupying higher position represent her most important goals which she works strenuously to realize furtively despite her beautiful and idealistic talk about asceticism, good will and sincerity of intention and despite her pretention to be pious, righteous and Faithfull. IQBAL has no enthusiasm to study, take notes or achieve good result .She found in Hafsa the best assistant in taking lecture notes, summarizing references and syllabuses. Therefore their relationship becomes strong. They felt that they complete one another.

With her experience and skill, Hafsa was able to control political work in the branch of the party at the university. A rumor has spread about the elections being forged, that was why her party won the election and she became the president of the student union, and year after year her party was the sole winner in the election for the students union. She remained as presidents until she was graduated from the university, in the same way she had been skillful in her women organization at her area, she became skillful in coordinating students and implementing the party's secret plans and programs in the different faculties . She was also able to improve and develop her skill in writing reports analyzing the political situation and make political forecast to what is expected to come in the future, in short, she became a brilliant star in the world of politics . She was able to acquire the admiration of her seniors and was appointed manager of one of the party's secret organizations immediately after graduation from the university. As part of policy of the party in attracting the gifted individuals of the new generations she appointed a teacher in Madame Assam's school same as other party cadres who are appointed every year and distributed to school, hospitals, and different government institutions to control them. Since she did not want to be separated from IQBAL she exploited her extensive relations and appointed her as social instructor after persuading her that her job will be easy and comfortable and need little effort. They both obtained what they wanted but they unexpected presence of Ustaz JALAL in the school had been the commencement of problems between them on the one hand and him on the other hand. Ustaz JALAL who is known to be careful and keenly interested in the welfare of the school noticed the arrogance, negligence, carelessness and recklessness of the tow new comers. Although Hafsa was behaving as if she is the owner of the school but the problems of Ustaz JALAL with IQBAL has the lions share compared to his problems with Hafsa. Ustaz JALAL believes whole heartedly that IQBAL job is the most important job in the school but IQBAL spends most of her time in reading stories and women magazines. He started to argue with her quietly and gently to give more time and care for her job but when he noticed that carelessness and negligence are increasing he becomes more violent and severe. Such debates between them, diminishes her worth and weight in his eyes and at the same time makes something move in her inner self, some kind of anger and rage mixed with pain. She was not used to receive, all her past life criticism, blamer reproach from anyone, She felt pain because she know that he sees her inferior than any teacher in the school, perhaps if the source of pain is another person the effect will be deferent . She will not bother much. Ustaz JALAL is something else to her. With the passage of days she became wishful to become respectful in his eyes. She extended considerable effort to control herself so as to change his opinion about her but uselessly since he already took a law opinion about her actor discovering she was not qualified for her job, that any criticism or advice directed to her will be of no use and will add further complications. He has dropped her out of his mind convinced that the best thing to do is to leave her alone and carry out her work instead of her for the welfare of the students. He thought for a long time to find an alternative and at last he chose Samia, mathematics teacher to help him to shoulder the new responsibility and told her. She agreed at once for she had been watching silently like other teachers, how IQBAL is so apathetic about performing her job. Ustaz JALAL and Samia succeeded in solving many problems related to the students. Iqabal felt more angered. Her anger and pain converted to hate and animosity. She felt as if fire is kindled inside her towards Samia. The school year ended and summer holiday came, she felt irritated. She felt that this is the first holiday that comes in the wrong time. In the past she used to wait impatiently for the summer holiday take a captive released from his shackles. When she was alone during the holiday she thought much and became convinced that she is in bad need to change her style of life and behavior. When the new school year started, she made some effort to change her behavior and give more care her work but she failed to change Ustaz Jalal's outlook toward her, and attract his attention to herself. Therefore she resorted to objection against his interference in her job and performing it instead of her. Of course such interference wouldn't have bothered so much, had it not been accompanied with Samia interference. Doing her job on her behalf wouldn't annoy her a bit, but Samia and Ustaz Jalal getting closer to each other and having something common between them would annoy her very much. Ustaz JALAL did not give the least care about her objection .He continued to carry out Iqbla's duties although the headmaster advised him to keep away from IQBAL and her work as she could easily inflict harm on him through her father's influence. She was completely helpless to please him or stop Samia's interference. So she agreed upon Hafsas suggestion to file a complaint against him. Although she was convinced that what she is going to do is wrong and although she was not feeling at ease, but the jealousy which was kindled inside her made her agree to hafsa's suggestion in a desperate attempt to compel Ustaz JALAL to feel how important she is and that he must respect social status .Hafsa took this golden opportunity for which she waited a long time. On the one hand she will revenge from him, and on the other hand she will see more suffering and pain on IQBAL's countenance if he was transferred to another school. The gap of disagreement which is already broad will become broader, and this will bring more comfort and pleasure to her heart. So she hastened to send a complaint to the local office of the party informing the senior official in the office that Ustaz JALAL made the tow of them focus of attention with his continuous criticism, that he is working very hard to destroy the project they were implementing for the benefit of the party and that he is of the most fierce opposes of the government's policies. She added that he will definitely succeed in his efforts if he was not restrained. Immediately the local office sent representative to explain the situation to the director of the supervisory office which supervises Asma's School and several schools in the area, and order him to silence that teacher or substitute him by another teacher or dismiss him from common good. The director of the supervisory sent at once for Ustaz Jalal.

Ustaz JALAL went the supervisory office. He opened the door and introduced himself to the secretary who permitted him to enter the director's office. When he opened the door he was struck by a cool air emitted by tow air conditioner fixed on the wall opposite to the door. He smelt a nice smell, a mixture of piercing perfume and oriental incense. He felt he is regaining his concentration, even he that part of concentration which was shattered by scorching heat outside and the noise and crowdedness of transportation. He stepped leisurely on the precious Turkish carpet crossing the distance of the five meters which separate the long ebony table of the office room, and sat on one of the opposite chairs close to the table, the tow chairs were separated by a small curved glass table on which was put with marble vessel full of different types of natural flowers .The man behind the elegant office pointed to him to sit uninterrupted his telephone conversation. He turned his eyes from the rosy- cheeked, light beard, sharp – sighted, young – faced man who was wearing a transparent Italian glasses and who seem to e living in luxury and comfort, to the glittering furniture which is all made of imported wood and smiled sarcastically when he remembered the slogans of the ruling party about self –sufficiency which this party kept reiterating for years in information media day and night calling for stopping importation and reliance and local production . His sarcastic smile broadened when he saw a charming golden frame in which was written in Arabic Kufic letters ((work is trust)). Then triple writing ((justice is the foundation of rule)), his thought were interrupted by the voice of the young man who put back the telephone receiver and said coldly:

- "Welcome Ustaz Jalal??
- Yes welcome to you" replied Ustaz JALAL.
  The directors voice rose and asked again more coldly.
- Ustaz Jalal??
- Yes " he replied
  The young man turns the pages of a file carefully.
- You have an extant service record why do you want lose it for nothing?

Ustaz JALAL – who until now does not know why he was summoned, ignored the threatening pitch which is quite conspicuous in the speaker's voice and words. He was surprised. He asked;

13

- What makes me to lose it?

- Your endless problems, your continuous interference in things not of your concern and obstructing the work of your colleagues.

He realized at once that the matter is related to Hafsa and IQBAL. He asked in a sarcastic voice.

- What colleagues are you talking about?

- You know quite well about whom am I talking, we do not want more problems, so I tell you flatly if you want to remain in your job, do not interfere, in any form, in the affairs of your school colleagues, mind your own business, do your duties, and nothing more .

He became angry that this arrogant person dares to talk to him so insolently. The absurdity of the superintendent increased his anger but he controlled himself and smiled saying:

- It is part and parcel of my duty as deputy headmaster to try to solve the problems which occur in the school. Moreover, those about what you are talking understand nothing about their duties. In addition to that they care nothing about school and those in the school; they have other tasks which they do for other quarters. I despise the method of threat and intimidation. If my job will silence me from saying the truth and farce me to abandon my duty, then good bye this job, take me away from it if you like . At least I will not feel sad because I know that those who control education is a group of a large – fisted gangs who raise their fists in the face of poor and weak people to silence their voices. that is the only thing they are good at "

The face of the superintendent becomes white while listening to Ustaz JALAL who continued his speech quietly;

- "Until I lose my job, I will do what I see right and serve the welfare of the school and the students ", for it is a trust that God will ask me about.

Before listening to what the astonished superintendent are going to say he stepped towards the door feeling as if the air conditioners had halted suddenly and the large office room is getting smaller and its walls coming closer as if they are going to fold and stifle his breath. Although the air was hot outside but he felt some kind of ease and comfort.

Ustaz JALAL already knew that favoritism and corruption have spread in all government institutions, that the criteria of appointment in jobs are no longer the ability and efficiency but intercession and recommendation by influential persons.

He was hoping that corruption shall not reach the field of education because education in his opinion is something pure, sublime and even sacred that must keep away from any dirty practices. He believes that if education collapsed the whole nation will collapse. He thought that however the officials in charge of education are corrupted, yet they undoubtedly realize the importance of education and they will not risk forsaking it for political maneuvers and interests. He was convinced that there is nothing tempting in education which makes them control it or interfere in it. It is very strange that Madame Asama's School remained safe from any kind of direct interface all the past years. But with the passage of time he came to realize that what he was hoping for is more imagination or even delusion. Things remained all right until Hafsa and Iqpal joined the school.

When he observed how they gave no weight for the school laws and regulations,an overwhelming wrath possessed him not against them only but basically against the senior officials in charge of education as they are ready to do anything to realize their ends .

Wrath inside him was increasing and escalating day after day. He reached the climax of indignation when he met the superintendent of education whom he regards as one of the tools of tampering with education. That was why she said what he has said to him although he knew very well that what he has said will be a sufficient reason for his dismissal. He knew that that will take this opportunity to get rid of him and throw him in the street .After all, this is their way and style in doing things. Once you disagree with them, they take the first chance to throw you away. Either you be with them and obtain everything or against them and obtain nothing. Perhaps he realized that he may be exposed to more than just dismissal from work... a car may come in the darkness of the night and take him to an unknown place and only God knows whether he will come back home or not . Therefore he kept thinking about what might happen to him and how to get along with his family responsibilities after his father's death.

Their share from income of the plot of land cultivated by his uncle at their village will not be sufficient to meet the requirements of the family which are increasing day after day. He is not skilled in any other occupation, and even if he wants to practice any other job they will be put obstacles on his way ... there is a whole year remaining before his brother graduates from the university. And even after leaving the university nobody knows when he will find a job... They may punish his brother by shutting all the doors of work before him to revenge from Ustaz Jalal.

He kept all the way thinking about what he can do. When he reached the gate of the school he felt that he needs to telephone his nephew who works abroad and who kept all the way thinking about what he can do. When he reached the gate of the school he felt that he needs to telephone his nephew who works abroad, and who kept for several years requesting him to join him but he kept refusing that offer in spite of the various benefits that he promised him to reap in a short time because he loves his homeland more than any other country in the world, because he loves his occupation as teacher more than any other occupation and because the sky in which he can see the moon acre scent than a half moon, then a full moon, and which he can see the clouds drawing cottages, faces, birds and naked laughing children is lovable to him than himself .

[3]

Salma stood in front of her father's house very exhausted knocking the door weakly after walking all that long distance from school to her home in the scorching heat of the afternoon. She was listening patiently to the voice of her step mother saying disgustedly after every knock,

- "Oh, wait a little … "

She knew that her step mother knew who is knocking the door. So she deliberately delays opening it. She does that most every day. Salma kept waiting for a long time despite the severe heat and thirst which burns her empty stomach. At least Ikhlass face appeared stained and boiled, as usual with dyes of different colors, smiling sarcastically and asking ironically:

- "Is it you who has been knocking … I thought you are another person … ha …ha … haaaaay - Laughing that long impudent laugh - Welcome, welcome, very very, very welcome.

Salma entered without uttering a word. She knew that any word might drag her into more troubles.

The house is composed of two rooms, one of them occupied by her father and step mother, and the other occupied her and her tow half brothers towards whom she feel no brotherly emotion . The same room is also used for receiving the guests and visitors. This room which is built with clay and burnt brick, roofed with dom tree stems, straw mats and hay and painted from inside with green color is often converted to a saloon for receiving guests . And if the guest is a man Salma had to sleep in the small kitchen with pots, plates, dishes and the washing basin in winter. In summer she used to sleep at the small space in front of the kitchen. In this case she had to spend the night under the watchful eye of Ikhlas her step mother. She prefers the dishes and the washing basin. Therefore she often even in the summer, sleeps in the kitchen despite the severe heat and ugly smell of burnt wood and dry dough and despite the wet ground due to overflow of dirty water from the washing basin ....

On her way to her room, she passed by the tow zeers (water pots) placed on an iron stand in the middle of the main courtyard.

She took the aluminum cup from the wooden cover from one of the tow zeers, filled the cup and drank some water.

She felt the water descending cold to her empty stomach and felt a piercing pain. She put back the cover on the zeer and the cup on the cover and walked to her room to drop her old worn out school bag, change her school uniform, go the kitchen to eat something as she didn't eat anything since the morning, then go back to the room to take some rest after the long walk to and from the school .But once she reached to the door of her room, she was astounded to find the small cupboard, in which she keeps her clothes, some of her school books and the only photograph of her mother, was wide open although she left it closed in the morning .. Her books were torn and put on the windows and bed, her modest clothes were scattered on the ground, her under – clothes were spread everywhere, and her mother photograph was torn into two halves and covered with dust. When she saw all this, her bag fell from her hand. She stood struck for awhile looking at her books and clothes as if frozen. A mixture of different feelings came over her ... a kind of shame for the sight of her scattered under were clothes an overwhelming worth, helplessness, oppression and pain. She suddenly jumped, picked up the photograph, cleared it from the dust and held it to her breast, then she knelt to collect her clothes and torn out books feeling week and helpless. She put them back in the small old cupboard and closed it again, then dropped herself on the bed weeping bitterly and painfully. She knew who are the culprits and the person who incited them to do so. The offenders are her brothers. They are used to take every opportunity to injure her, and their mother is used to instigate them against her, cultivate her hatred in their hearts and push them to insult her and revenge from her. They always respond to their mother in a way that makes Salma ask herself often whether they are really her brother's flesh and blood. she was very tired, sad, thirsty and hungry, she didn't exactly knows when and how she slept, but she awake suddenly, a hand was shaking her violently, when she opened her eyes she saw the frowning face of her step mother with its ugly days and bright yellowish colors addressing her severely " wake up, the house needs cleaning and the clothes of the two boys need washing, this permanent routine that Salma has to do daily.

Ikhlas hated salma long before she came to live with her as she had hated Salma's mother. Ikhlas was brought up with Ahmed, Salma's father in the same residential quarter. Despite the huge difference between her lower class family, she spend a large portion of her child and girlhood with Ahamed's family which is composed of Ahmed parents and two sisters Safa and Hanaa . When she was a child, she used to spend most of the day in that large beautiful house playing and watching the television. She always refuse to go back to her family's house, which is a few meter distance from Ahamd's house unless coerced by her mother crying and shouting, or sleeping carried on her mother's shoulders, sometimes her mother would leave her to stay as she like upon the insistence of Ahmed mother to let her play as much as possible, and since she is never satisfied of playing, she never goes home by herself. Therefore her mother would find herself compelled to go to Ahmed's home at the end of each day to bring her back home. If she finds her sleeping, she would carry her easily to their house, but if she happens to be awake, all her attempts to convince her go back home would fail. So she finds no other alternative than carrying her will and desire. Then she would start crying and shouting as if she is expelled from paradise to hell. She would never stop crying until she is overcome by sleep. She would then sleep with her tears on her cheeks.

Ikhlas passed quickly from the stage of childhood to adolescence like many girls at that time. Her emotional attachment to the big house and its inhabitants has increased. She started to feel something attract her to Ahmed and strongly desire to see him whenever he is out of her sight. If she meets him casually, she would blush while this wouldn't have bothered her the least in the past. What was previously quite ordinary, now become a strong thing that makes her face rosy, her heart beat violently and her mind troubled and perplexed. Seeing him stealthily makes her full of secret joy and pleasure, a sort of joy unknown to her before, unlike the joy of innocent playing which she thought as more loveable to her than anything in her life. Her concern about him grew bit by bit without being felt by anyone else. She would a kind of happiness that cannot be described whenever she helps Hanaa and Safaa in doing anything related to him such as participating in preparing or ironing his clothes or tidying his room and sometimes volunteer to do these things by her. She became over attached to him until she thought, mistakenly, that he has the same feeling for her to the extent that she started to interpret his behavior and every word he utters in a way that satisfy her feeling and satiate her feverish desire and great craving to hear any word of praise from him . She released the rein to her imagination and delusions. With the passage of days the feeling that Ahmed is hers alone increased. She began to believe that she is the only girl in the world who is worth of Ahmed. The only person who has the right to serve him and would feel jealous if anybody rendered a little service to him. That inordinate passion was combined with girlish dreams that have no ground accompanied by another trend of thinking about the life of luxury she shall enjoy, the big house she will live in, the car which will be at her disposal and the immense fortune that will become her if she married him. She was absorbed in her dreams and therefore she neglected her study and only completed the intermediate school. She did not think of carrying out any work to help her poor family. She doesn't like reading. That is why her intellectual faculties remained limited and narrow, she devoted her whole life for her dreams. She spent most of her time between the house of Ahmed family and the other house's in her residential quarter especially during the different events and occasions that occur from time to time such as wedding, birth, circumcision and death. Although she enjoys gathering of people in one place even if the occasion is a sad one like the death of a close friend or a dear relative but her feeling of joy multiplies if the reason of the gathering is a wedding since wedding ceremonies usually gather a large number of people than other occasions and therefore she would have the opportunity to meet relatives and friends who had been absent for a long time. She habitually feel elated since the first preparation for the wedding such as tailoring wedding dresses, making pastry and confectionery, purchase and mixing of perfumeries and dying feet and hands with henna, accompanied with girls songs. Her feeling of happiness increases and reaches its climax on the wedding day itself when the place becomes like a beehive and her name is reiterated among the audience requesting her to do this and that or asking her about something related to the wedding . She is fond of rendering services to the wedding guests. Since she was a girl, she was expected to become an excellent house wife and reliable to do many things requiring special skills related to housewifery. Therefore it is quite normal that she is often assigned carry out several and various tasks during ceremonies. This makes her always needed, happier, more pleasant, excessively joyful – and self – confident. But when people gather around the bride her happiness dissipates and jealousy come over he making her overwhelming desiderate if she could replace bride even if the bride is her friend or sister. She would feel a sort of heavy and deep dejection. This feeling usually starts with first person to departure from the wedding house and an increase gradually at the departure of the last person to reach it is climax when she herself leaves the wedding house. She usually remains until the last moments to sip the last drop of happiness whose source is the gathering of people in the same place. The hardest moment comes when she departs from the wedding house and say farewell to the inhabitants of the wedding house before returning home. She always goes to the ceremonies in high sprit and departs in low spirit. The dispersal of people after their gathering always makes her feel depressed. Although she tried many times to get rid of this feeling but she always fails. After the end of each occasion, she always feels a great deal o f voidness and loneliness. She will not recover from this state unless several days pass and after relating the details of the occasion to Hanaa and Safaa many times ever if they attended the occasion.

Things went on like this until Safaa and Hanaa were married and left the big house. She felt more emptiness after the marriage of the two sisters but she found a justification to stay as much as possible in Ahmed's home with the pretext of helping his mother who found in her compensation` for her daughters. Therefore she depended on her in many tasks. This made her feel more entitled to Ahmed and she began to behave like a wife who makes her best to please her husband. With the passage of days she became definitely convinced that becoming Ahmed's wife is only a matter of time and she will leave to the big house permanently... But Ahmed whom she remained dreaming of all these years, and thought he -likes her as she like him and built all her hopes on the basis of his presence in her life, has not the least feeling towards her, he is unknown of her thoughts and plans. He is quite engrossed in his successful career and private life. He does not notice who irons his clothes or tidy his room. Ikhlas is not the kind of girls that excite his interest, draw his attention or capture his thoughts. He was infatuated with layla, Salmas mother who was his maternal residential quarter was blossoming like a young rose. Everything in her was just as dreamt of and for ... her charming beauty, excellent morals and behavior, her reason and logic, her attractive modesty and quietude... But Ahmed hid his love even from layla itself. He kept waiting until the right time came and he became sure that layla loves him as he loves her. He soon told his parents who agreed and was pleased with his choice. Then he betrothed her. Ikhlas did not believe when she heard about his intention to betroth layla. Her mind refused the news totally as if she didn't hear. She remained unbelieving until the engagement was announced officially. She tried to specifically that he is not going to marry a girl other than herself ... perhaps he engaged layla to please his mother or father on any other person and he will leave layla and come back to her. She continued to deceive herself like any other failing lover whose beloved abandoned her suddenly. She came to cling to false hopes and ungrounded illusions to pacify her trembling heart and ameliorate the burden of pain on her shocked soul. When she was certain that Ahmed's marriage to loyal was concluded, she fell ill shivering silently save for suppressed grumbles and few uncontrollable words, the traitor, the thief, the car, money ... etc raving with these words, repeating them over and over and shaking violently like epileptic. when the fit of fever gets severe, she loses self control, her breath accelerates, her eyes bulge, and her body trembles as if her spirit is about to leave her body . They took her to the doctor who was unable to diagnose her case and gave her some medicines to sedate the fever. Upon the insistence of one of her relatives, they took her to Sheikh Ali who assured them that she is enchanted by an evil eye but she will soon recover if they followed his instructions. He gave them an amulet and number of folded paper filled incense. She used them but did not improve... She, alone knows the cause of her illness. She also knows that it is difficult to cure it.

Therefore she stayed in bed undesired to recover wishing to die but she did not die. She remained in bed for a long time and all people became at a loss with regards to her illness.

Her mother was the only person who stayed close to her days and night trying to display patience when her daughter is conscious and weep silently when Ikhlas is attacked by a fit of fever, and becomes unconscious and disclose all her secrets.

[4]

On one Thursday late afternoon, when the sun was about to set, and the red light of the evening twilight was infiltrating through the crack of her small wooden window the bed in which she was lying and the voices of the children who were playing football rose with shrill shouts and gay laughter, Ikhlas heard low knocks at the outer door which is made of zinc plate fixed by long nails on horizontal and vertical pieces of wood. She dropped he ears to hear more conspicuously ... the fits of fever had departed two days ago, she was feeling quietude and tranquility of emotionally wounded persons who cry for long hours and dry up their tears and their sadness dissipates . It is seldom that somebody knocks their outer door as it is always open. Mostly, they are visited by relatives and neighbors who enter directly through the open door to the small courtyard and raise their voices saying Salmu Alaikum (peace be upon you) as a notification that they entered the sanctuary of the house. Therefore she expected the visitor to be stranger. There was no body in the house expect her mother washing the dishes in the kitchen. A moment of silence had passed, and then she heard her mother's voice welcoming the visitor warmly, then the voice of Ahmed and his father exchanging the welcoming words with her mother and asking her if they could see her. She did not believe her ears. Ahmed father visited her twice before but this is the first time Ahmed visits her .When she heard his voice, she felt that all her pains had vanished, a wave of sudden joy engrossed her heart and its beat accelerated lightly and violently, her weakness which why caused by the successive fits of fever and her abstention to take food had disappeared, in less than a moment she sat straight in bed. She took the water cup from the small table beside her, washed her face quickly, and collected her scattered disheveled hair and tied it at the back of her head, then lied on her back and drew the blanket on her body leaving only her face . While he was shaking hands with her, she felt as though an electric charge was creeping and spreading all over her feeble body was providing her with more strength and vital experiencing. The same feeling when she heard his voice at first. She was quite silent looking shyly at him from time to time while he was talking with her mother trying to assure her that she is getting well and will soon recover. Despite her conviction that he knew he strong attachment to him and that he wanted her as she wanted, she didn't feel any animosity or hatred towards him. She never felt that he betrayed or deserted her. She didn't feel that he was blamable or the contrary, She lied all the blame on Layla. She has a terrible hatred and a bitter malice towards her. She wished if he wouldn't leave her room for ever but time passed so quickly. They took permission and left the room. Her mother accompanied them to the outer door. She sat straight in the middle of the bed thinking, why she wishes to die? Why did she submit so easily? Why did she leave another girl interior than steal the dream of her life and marry the only man she wished to share her life with she allowed layla to take Ahmed from her to live happily with him. Layla must have deceived him. She must have done far more than this to tempt him to marry, suddenly an idea came to her mind like a flash of lightening .Layla must have conspired with a Sheikh to enchant him to abandon me and marry her. Certainly she did that or else why did he abandon me and married her although he knew that I would do the impossible to please him ... how stupid was I not to think of this matter in this way before!! Don't I hear everyday stories about the women in her residential quarter with religious Sheiks? Didn't Saadiaa, daughter of Mohammed, marry the man who wished to marry after the train of marriage had over passed her and after waiting long years for him to come back and marry her although, before he went away, he had no intention to marry her after all people thought that he will never come back . Wasn't the Sheikh able to separate Miriam, Ismail's daughter from the betrothed Osama after Mardia, who wanted to marry him, went to the Sheikh and married Osama after two weeks although she was older than him? Strangely enough he broke his engagement to Miriam without any apparent reason? Wasn't he able to make Buthayna, daughter of Suliman, give birth to a child after ten years of her marriage and after ordering her to slaughter a ram and distribute the meat to the poor people? Didn't they manage to rejoin Amouna, daughter of Ahmed, to her husband who divorced her and swore that he will never remarry her after mistreating, humiliating, pulling his mothers hair and slapping her on her face until she fell down . Didn't the Sheikh cure Zakyia, daughter of khalil the tinker, after he fellow wife conspired with another Sheikh to paralyze her? Wasn't the Sheikh able to make the husband of Alawyia Toms daughter like the ring of her finger whereas he had been before like a fierce lion, and he is quite docile, submitting to her opinions and decisions, responding to all her demands and not doing anything without taking her permission not only this but also boycotted his brother and deserted his parents home to please hers. Didn't Mammon divorce his wife Maria, whom he loved so much and was ready to do anything for her sake after his mother conspired with Sheikh Eluryan to make her son hate his wife? Both Maria and their children became most hateful in his eyes; He abandoned them as if he did not know them before. It is even said that the reason Abdu's lunacy who walk naked, sleeps in the streets, and eat with animals is due to his wife's conspiracy with Sheikh Elqadban to make abdue lose his mind because he married another women.. Verily sheikh can do anything and layla must have gone to one of them to enable her to get married to Ahmed. How stupid and how helpless was she to sit waiting silently thinking that he loves her as she loves him, leaving layla to steel him from her by means of a Sheik . But aren't Sheiks available now? Then why should she submit? Why shouldn't she fight her enemy with the same weapon? Couldn't she go to a Sheikh to take her revenge, it is unfair to give up because Ahmed is her alone... She must do anything to regain him. If she is unable to do so, she should, at least, take her revenge instead of leaving him to that thief to live her life with him ... layla the traitor, the evil. She should now leave her bed and try as hardly as possible to get Ahmed back to her life. And keep him away from layla by any means. From now on she mustn't refuse to take food and lie in bed helplessly and desperately... Despair is of no avail. She felt great comfort. She was overwhelmed by a curious determination and a tremendous desire to revenge. This has supplied with more strength. For the first time since her illness, her voice came out weakly calling her mother, who nearly fainted out of astonishment asking her to bring her some food. In a few days, IKhlas was able to leave her bed and start her journey to Sheiks and tombs. She is optionally entering a strange world whom she knew nothing about save for the stories and tales she has often heard her neighbors and relatives narrating about this mysterious world.

[5]

When Ahmed married Layla and she came to live with him in the large house, each of them realized how lucky he / she are to have such a partner. Each of them did his best to make the other happy. They were an ideal example of successful marriage. Marriage, familiarity, close affinity and nice mutual treatment and respect polished their feelings and increased their love for each other. After only two years Layla gave birth to Salma who came a facsimile of her charming tender and beautiful mother and added a new kind of happiness to the already happy home. He cannot stand being away from her ever for a short time. He used to go work in the morning but when he comes back at noon, he feels as if he was absent from home for days. When Salma was tow years old they decided to have another child. Layla was eager to beget a boy like Ahmed in everything. But while she was dreaming and planning to realize her dear wish, she felt a slight pain which she thought to be transient and will soon disappear and there is no need go to the doctor . Although the pain increased, she tried to be patient so as not to make Ahmed and his parents anxious or worried. The pain escalated that within only few days she became unable to rise from her bed and Ahmed hastened to take her t the doctor, who, after carefully medical examination was not able to diagnose her case advised him to make a comprehensive laboratory examination but when he brought the results the doctor told him that they are all clean. He took her a -number of famous consultant doctors who unanimously agreed that her case is very strange and she has no visible disease. Ahmed became puzzled and seriously worried. He couldn't understand what was going on around him. She was burning and perishing like a candle. One of his close friends, who were a doctor, advised him to take her abroad were medical experience and equipment is far better there. He hurriedly applied for a leave from work and started to race with time to obtain exit visas for him and Layla but days passed without achieving anything. His application was rejected without any explanation although he produced more than ten medical reports confirming the urgent need of his wife to travel abroad for treatment. In spite of his extensive relations and mediations of his acquaint ants he failed to get the required exit visas. He tried to know the reason of this rejection but vainly, the chairman of the medical committee assigned to look into applications of travelling abroad for medical treatment was a young man in his early thirties. The previous chairman of the committee was a famous surgeon- who was dismissed for common good. He has refused many generous offers to work for famous private and public hospitals abroad because he preferred to sever his country and use his knowledge for benefit of the helpless citizens who are in bad need for him. That young man has no connection what saver with either doctors or the science of medicine. His overwhelming enthusiasm drove him to reject all application submitted to the committee with pretext that the country is full of well equipped hospitals and competent doctors equal to most excellent doctors in the world although these applications and reports were issued by the same hospitals and doctors he is referring to . However his rejection was not emanating from ill intention or wickedness but emanating of ignorance and arrogance which is usually inflict decision makers in the developing countries as well as blind fanaticism which make him see everything national as perfect. He believes that anything national is better than anything foreign .Whether human beings, animals, birds, or even insects, plants, rivers, forests and mountains .... Etc.

Ahmed was about to be mad seeing Layla approaching death without being able to do anything to save her life. Ikhlas heard about Ahmed's attempts to accompany Layla abroad for treatment. She Endeavour's might succeed. She had visited a number of tombs and many Sheikhs to help her to separate Ahmed and Layla. But she kept going from Sheikh to Sheikh after the previous Sheikh burdens her with the endless demands starting with small amounts of money. Escalating gradually to become exorbitant a mounts. Although the amounts of money demanded by Sheikhs varied from one Sheikh to another, yet they all agreed that what she wants is difficult to do and needs a lot of money, time and effort. She was about to be desperate until she found Sheikh Ali. She had heard about him and his extraordinary abilities at a funeral ceremony. She asked about his address and immediately went to his house in one of the poor residential quarter at the outskirts of the city hoping that he will be better than the previous Sheiks she had been used to visit. Once she entered the small room which was built with clay. and on whose walls were fixed pieces of different wild animals skins separated by strange devilish drawing, she was convinced that she, at last found the man she had been searching for and she became more convinced when he called her by her name before introducing herself and told her about the reason of her visit . He even asked about her mother leg pain. She did not stay along with him and he didn't demand anything from her but promised her that Loyla will be inflicted with a kind of illness impossible to be cured. He also told her that Ahmed will look after Loyla at the beginning and will try his best to treat her but he will soon divorce her. He asked her to visit him after Loyla divorce. All his predictions came to be true. Layla fell ill and all attempts to make her recover had failed. But should she wait until Ahmed take layla abroad for treatment. She didn't whether Sheikh Ali's powers could extend reach Layla abroad to prevent her from being cured. Layla may be cured and all her efforts would be wasted. The best thing to do is to go back to Sheikh Ali as quickly as possible to tell him about the last developments. She must leave anything to circumstances. In the small clay room she told Shiekh about her fears and beseeched him to something to prevent Ahmed and Layla from going abroad. He looked at her for a long time. She felt her body shudder from this strange look .He then time turned his look away from her, closed his eyes, raised his head up and set his legs apart, then fearful voice came out from his mouth, then he stretched his hands as if he is going to wrestle something invisible, then she heard strange violent shouts of unknown source. She felt terrified. Terror filled her body. She was about to run away but she couldn't move, then the shots changed to painful groans like the groans of somebody suffering the agony of death, then everything became calm . Sheikh Ali opened his eyes slowly as if he is experiencing a tremendous pain, then he told her in a terrible calm voice that there is only one way to realize what she wants, and that way will make Layla unable to leave her bed ever, then remained silent for a few minutes then asked her whether would agree to that way, and whether she is ready to respond to all his demands. She kept silent for a long time. She was hesitant and was about to refuse his offer. This is the first time for her to be the cause of harm to anybody. But is she refused Sheikh Ali's offer. Layla may go abroad and recover, and in this case she has to start again from zero pain and she wasn't sure whether she will succeed or fail ... No she can't wait more than this to defeat her enemy. Moreover, since this is in a war and there is no war without a victims. She mustn't allow Layla to defeat her again. Hasn't Layla murdered her when she stole Ahmed from her? Hasn't she lied in bed wishing every moment to die? Didn't she swear before that she will do anything to separate Layla from Ahmed? She felt that she became possessed by wrath and malice and so she expelled her fears and promised Sheikh Ali that she is ready to do anything he wants from her.

[6]

Ikhlas executed to the orders of Sheikh Ali literally .She kept away from water and cleanliness, did not pray for three days, drank the jet block, bitter and ugly smell liquid on the fourth day, wrapped the empty bottle with pages from the Holy Quran and threw it in the latrine. On the fifth day layla died. Ikhlas rejoiced and was about to dance out of happiness while other women around her were crying and shouting from the shock of Laylas death. Ahmed was overwhelmed with sadness. Everything became black in his world which was saturated with his great love for his dear wife. He remained distracted for a long period. Some people thought that he will soon lose his mind. All people around him made strenuous efforts to pull him out of this state of mind. They reminded him of Salma and her need for his care and love after losing her mother. He came to his mind gradually. Funeral days passed and people ceased to come to the big house so as to mind their own businesses. Life will never stop for the death of anyone whoever he or she might be. He became deeply dejected engrossed in his work to forget his calamity and pains but a puzzling question kept revolving in his mind torturing and adding more dejection and agony to his tormented heart. He kept asking himself why didn't they allow him to travel abroad to save his poor wife? What crime did he commit to receive such an inhuman treatment? He has no relationship whatsoever with politics. Since a student and up to now, he had not the least interest in the world of politics and politicians. He devoted himself to his studies when he was a student and for his work after graduation from the university. After marriage he devoted most of his time to his small family. Even his father has no political activity. His business as a rich and successful merchant preoccupied all his time. Then why did they prevent him from going abroad and by doing so they killed his wife deliberately and destroyed his happiness. Over and above he knew very well that his mother was suffering more than him particularly when she sees him so silent, distracted and absent minded. That is why he would often leave the house and refuge to the Nile bank where he ruminates his pains alone to her. He would deliberately stay there to make sure that she is a sleep, and then he would come back and sneak furtively to his bed. But his mother realizes why he always escapes from home and why he is always late. She could never sleep before he comes back and would wait torn out with fears, anxiety and solicitude .She developed the habit of watching him silently and patiently hoping that time will cure his pains and make him forget and revert as he was before Laylas death, pleasant, optimistic, joyful, bloomy and always smiling sweetly . But years passed without any change. His isolation, introversion, loneliness and depression continued to increase day after day. His mother, who kept watching him, torn – hearted for theses years since Layals death, spoke with his father about his pitiable condition. They both agreed that nothing could pull him out of this wretchedness than a new wife to compensate him and encompass him with tender love and kind sympathy, his mother took the opportunity of a quiet hour and approached him about getting married again but he apologized that he cannot marry at present and requested to postpone talking about this matter for the time. She decided to wait for some time then talk to him again and again. She insisted that it is better for him to marry but in vain. He told her that he cannot marry again and that he decided to dedicate his life to his daughter. She became really anxious and sad about him but could do nothing. Ahmed's love and faithfulness were not the only reason for his determination not to remarry. He has strong belief and conviction that there is no women in the whole world who could bring up a child of another women with love, mercy sympathy and passion as his true mother, and no women could respond to his needs except hi own mother. Therefore, he had no intention whatsoever to bring a step mother who would torture and humiliate Salma. Thus his reply to his mother was decisive and final. One day he stayed for a long time on the Nile bank absorbed for in his past and memories until mid night. He was bewildered for sitting so long beside the River bank, He stood up hurriedly and started to cross the empty quiet and silent streets except for striding of a cockroach, howling of a dog or croaking of frog until he arrived home... he entered and closed the outer door quietly … he walked stealthily and cautiously towards his room but before he reached it he passed closely near his mothers and was anguished to see her weak body shaking, and hear her crying voice under her blanket. He knew that he is the cause of her tears. He did not leave her and embraced her, pacified her and wiped off her tears. He did not leave her until she become quite quite. Then he went to his room and lye in his bed blaming and reproaching himself till the morning. What is her crime to deserve all this pain, torture and anguish? It is her right as any mother to see him happy and joyful and it is his duty to look after and make sure that she is quite happy and contented. Her age and fragile body cannot endure tension, anxiety and pain. He was selfish to think only about himself and the interest of his daughter. His fear about his daughter made him although he knows very well how she dedicated her life for making happy. He felt that he committed a grave unpardonable crime making her wretched and miserable. There is only one thing which could make her recover happiness and peace of mind and he is determined to do it whatever it might cost him. He will marry for the sake of her comfort, safety and tranquility. As for Salma she is still young and her grandmother will not give her up. Soon.

Next morning he and his mother sat at small table to drink tea before he leaves home for work. He said smiling without introduction he said:

"I have decided to marry. His mother nearly disbelieved him, but embraced him while her tears were flowing from her eyes down her cheeks. She felt as though a heavy burden is removed from her heart. the real motive of this decision is what had happened last night between them and realized that it was not taken by him out of conviction and contentment, but she was deadly confident that a new loving wife can pull out her beloved son from the abyss of his sadness and pain even if his motive behind marriage is not desire or love.

[7]

After Laylas death Ikhlas did her best to serve Ahmed's family. All people admired and praised her enthusiasm, faithfulness and goodness. She seldom leaves the big house and for a short time. She insisted that no one of Ahmed's family must do anything during all the period of the funeral days. She focused on giving her utmost care and attention to Ahmed's mother. She moved from place to place in the big house like a bee, receiving the women who to come to the house to the extent that all who does not know her thought she is one of the members of the family . She was extremely happy to do all the work. Despite her apparent and pretended sadness, She felt a great inner sensation of ease, comfort, rejoice and relaxation. She was full of hope that at last, with the death of her rival, she is definitely going to realize her aspirations. The way now is open to marry Ahmed, life is beginning to smile to her and her long suffering will soon come to an end. Although she was able to gain the confidence and love of Ahmed's family she failed to acquire Ahmed's love and confidence. However, she thought the matter require a little bit of patience and some time, but days, months and even years passed without achieving the least progress . She became impatient and started once again to search for Sheikh Ali who left his old house and went to live in another residential quarter. She asked many people to show her where he lives. After long search, she was able to find his new house but was told by his old neighbors' that he left about three months ago. After a week, she, at last, found Sheikh Ali. Three years had passed since their last meeting but he has not changed a bit, and so is the room found him sitting. It is just a true copy of the small clay room in which she saw him sitting when she met him for the first time in his previous house. He looked at her for a long time while she was entering the room. Her breast became compact, her buttocks became rounded, and all her physique became sexier than when he first saw her. He was extremely attracted to her since they first met. Therefore, he refused to take any money from her and requested to see her again not as assign of good will but because he knew, with his vast experience with all sorts of women that Ikhlas is that kind of women whom he could make like the ring of his finger with alight effort . Generally Sheikh Ali is excessively fond of women particularly young virgin girls. He is conjecture never fails to detect the easily seduced type of women. There is, inside him, something like a fire alarm or a compass pointer. Once a woman or a girl of the kind he knows he could undoubted seduce sits before him and starts to talk while he is looking fixedly in her eyes, that pointer would immediately begin to oscillate and vibrate . When he saw Ikhlas for the first time, he felt the pointer oscillating and shaking violently as though it was going to explode inside his bowels but, at that time he was preoccupied in devouring another prey. And now she came back after he was about to forget he. She became mature, sweeter and more feminine, just the type he prefer most. He must keep lied to him until he quenches his burning desire. All these thoughts revolved in his mind while he was receiving and welcoming her warmly. She was very pleased to have such a delighting reception and started to tell him how she was about to despair during her exhauster search to locate his house. She told him about her the failure of her hopes and attempts to marry Ahmed although three years had passed since the death of his wife. He listened to her attentively as he used to with women in general while trying to work out devilish plans to make them fall in his trap exploiting the minute details of the private secret which they disclose to him upon his insistence and that they must do so if they want to obtain what they want. When she finished, he decided to repeat with her the same old game he used to play with other women. He asked her to give him a period of grace for a week to consult his jinn servants about her case. She came back exactly after a week. He gave her some folded papers and asked her to burn them at any place in Ahmed's house and come back after a week. She returned on the appointed time. Once more he gave her similar papers and do the same with them as she did with the previous papers and come back this, she gave her a red liquid and ordered her to put a small amount of it, secretly in a cup of water or any other drink, mix it well, present it to Ahmed and make sure that he drinks it all. Then mix the remaining liquid with water, wash her chest with mixture and return after three days. She waited for three days. When she came back, he told her to come back after another week. She felt very tired, exhausted, and restless, depressed weary, trouble – minded and overstressed. But while she is with hum listening to his encouraging words, she would become full of hope, her despair would totally vanish, she became oscillating between hope and despair. Sheikh Ali deliberately started to keep her waiting for longer periods to make sure that she will soon lose patience and be prepared to respond to all his demands immediately without any hesitation. One evening she came to him sad, gloomy, miserable, bored, weary and harassed. When he saw her, he knew from the first moment that she has lost her patience, and can no longer stand waiting. The fruit is ripe and ready for him to pick. He closed his eyes as he usually does when he plans to delude or deceive somebody that his problem is intricate, complicated and very difficult to solve. Then he said tragically in solemn voice that her case is almost impossible to deal with since the magic Layla had used to bewitch Ahmed was composed of mixture of Indian witchcraft and red mercury whose effect is still deposited in Ahmed's belly in spite of the lapse of three years and there is only one way to spoil it and make Ahmed pay attention to her. Once more she felt her dream is fleeing, dissipating, shattering and scattering. She asked him – very confused – to explain more but he told her that he cannot tell her anything now and that she will knew everything when the right time comes. He added that if she agrees and he starts to work, she can neither withdraw nor refuse to do anything he demands from her; otherwise she will expose her life and the lives of those whom she loves to a great danger. She neither thought for long nor hesitated to tell him that she will not retreat and she is ready to respond to all his demands he knew that she is going to agree as many women did before her. He gave her three folded papers and asked her to put them one by one burning in censer, inhale their smoke just before sunset for three days go, directly to Ahmed's home on third day, and remain there until the Muezzin (announcer) of hours of prayer) call for the night prayer . He told her that on the fourth day she must wash herself, spray her body with some perfume, put on her most beautiful dress and come to his house without anybody knowing where she is going, then he warned her... Warning her – while putting the folded papers in her hand – that after using them in the way he described, she will never be able to retrocede and if she disobeyed him, she will bring condemnation mischief, troubles and suffering herself and all those around her. On the third day, just before sunset, Ikhlas went to the kitchen and kindled fire until the charcoal glowed red. when the smoke started to rise, she placed the small censer on the ground, stood over it, raised her dress to her lower thighs, separated them like an applause angle to allow the smoke to circulate all over her body – as described by Sheikh Ali – and remained sanding like this until the smoke disappeared. Then she hurried to Ahmed's home feeling for the first time, that she is taking the last step to overcome the deceased rival. On the fourth day she took her way to Sheikh Ali house in her full beauty and attractiveness but dominated by strange, hidden and unexplainable anxiety. She arrived at the poor squatter residential quarter where Sheikh Ali lives, went directly to the house and entered the small dark room which is crowded with strange devilish drawings. She inhaled the familiar smell of incense whose smoke fill until her eyes became familiar with the darkness and saw Sheikh Ali with eyes closed, his lips, moving without uttering any word while the beads of his rosary following each other between his forefinger and thumb in a monotonous movement and waving his head mechanically back and forward .

[8]

Ahmed simple and good – natured mother felt with her feminine instant – the covert desire of Ikhlas to marry her son and observed her persistent determination to realize her end. She noticed how she is keenly interested to serve and undertakes all things related to him. Consequently she is convinced that Ikhlas is going to be the suitable girl for Ahmed. All her son sufficient patience and consideration to bear his constant sadness and work hard to pull him out of his isolation and loneliness Ikhlas knew, feels, appreciates, and sympathize with all circumstances that surround him. She will certainly behave and deal with him from this background till he overcome his affliction. Therefore, his more exerted strenuous effort to attract her sons attention to Ikhlas by praising her abundantly whenever they sit together but all her attempts found no response from her son, however, she decided to talk to him frankly. Thus, on the day Ikhlas went to meet Sheikh Ali she prepared herself to talk to him. That day Ahmed came back late from work, she brought his dinner and set beside him while he was eating, then suddenly asked him:

– Have you found a bride or did you forget what we had agreed upon?

Actually he had forgotten the matter totally and not expected that his mother is going to approach him about it at this time, He answered her without thinking;

– I have not forgotten mother, but as you know, I have no time to select or search for a bride.

41

She knew he is trying to find an excuse but she decided to be decisive and leave him no way to escape. She said:

– How could you select a bride when you hardly talk to girls?

He dislikes talking about marriage therefore; he preferred to finish the conversation and said smiling:

– I will leave this matter to you mother. I trust any girl you choose will suit me perfectly, she wished if the girl he is going to marry will be of his own choice but she didn't want to let this opportunity escape from her. She said instantly :

– What do you think about Ikhlas?

Although he does not care whom she is going to select as his future wife, he was astonished and asked his mother:

– Ikhlas!! Ikhlas who?

His mother replied denyingly:

– What is the matter with you son? ... Ikhlas who does everything for you without feeling, let alone appreciation from your side ...Ikhlas who devote all her time for your service without you caring about her as if you are a stone ...

It is true that she is not so beauty but she is polite and faithful to our family ... Although she belongs to a poor family but they are decent people and good descent. Moreover, we know them since a long time ago. As our direct neighbors, they became quite familiar to us and so are we to them.

Her choice was surprise to him. He felt the morsel stop in his throat. He coughed repeatedly several times until tears filled his eyes. Insptie of his sadness, and although he didn't think of marriage at all after Laylas death, yet Ikhlas – specifically – is the last girl he could think of as a wife neither because she is not so beautiful, nor for the poverty of her family but because he believes she is not at all suitable for him as

42

they are different in everything. He was about to object but he said to himself "Ikhlas or any other girl, that makes no different after Layla had departed from this world. The women he loved had died. He will not find a woman like her ... he is not going to marry out of need or desire but because his mother wants him to, as long as his marriage will please his mother, why should he refuse the girl she had selected...

"Why don't you want to answer my question?

Her question pulled him out of his thoughts. He had been thinking it will be unfair for both him and Ikhlas to marry each other. However, he replied in a quiet voice "all right, ask her if she would agree to become my wife ".

–   "Ask her ..... Agree ...! You really seem to be quite unaware of what she has been doing to draw your attention to her, and how and why she has been careful to tend for your affairs all these years.

[9]

Ikhlas kept watching the rosary beads following each other monotonously between the fingers of Sheikh Ali who shut his eyes and continued to murmur whispering with his lips for a long time till she thought he is unaware of her presence and that she is sitting before him. She thought to make any sound to draw his attention to her presence but she could not dare to do so. She remained silent preferring not interrupt him while she is in such a condition otherwise he might be annoyed or even angry with her. She waited for a long time before he addressed her at last saying without opening his eyes and without halting the movement of the rosary between his fingers:

–   Come nearer to me – pointing to the forefront of the carpet on which he is sitting.

She was not surprised that he knew that it is she who is sitting with him in the small room without opening his eyes. No wonder she became accustomed to see him do many extraordinary things. She stood up, and then sat where he pointed to her until her knees were about to touch his knees .He bowed forward, stretched his hand and put it on her head pressing gently while still murmuring mysteriously. The pressure of his hand increased on her head. Suddenly his voice became louder and faster, he became breathless, his hand trembled nervously on her head, then all his body started to shake, shiver and quiver that she thought his argons are going to separate and shatter. Her heart was filled with fright and horror before he came to his senses, remove his hand from her head and demand her in an authoritative tone to uncover the upper part of her body. When he felt she is hesitant, he opened his reddish eyes, shot a harsh cruel look at her and said in a low but fearful cold voice:

- "Remember ... you had already promised to obey my jinn servants ... Be quick... Don't provoke their anger".

Then he closed his eyes again and raised his hand as if he is going to ward off – and invisible imminent danger from her. Driven by fear and desire to achieve her goal, she hastened to undress her upper part . He took a small amount of liquid from a clay pot beside him and started to rub her hair, neck and shoulder . Then his hand slipped to her breast she shuddered. She shuddered, became breathless and her face become congested .He stopped for a little while, took another vessel and ordered her to drink its contents. She started to drink and felt the biting, scorching white liquid descending down her stomach. His hand come again to her breast, neck and shoulders focusing specifically on the breast .She started to see things shaking and revolving around her and burning desire controlling all her body . Then her body became rumb. She was no longer able to sit straight... she leaned towards him ... He held her with hands, carried her and put her in a bed she had always asked herself about its presence in the small room as long as no one never uses it . Then she felt her clothes taken away from her body piece after piece without being able to move it a little bit. Although she was still conscious, she was quite motionless and vaguely aware of what was going around her. Although she was still conscious but she was quite motionless as if paralyzed. She was vaguely aware of what was going on around her. She felt the tough brown hand of Sheikh Ali moving feverishly up and down her body, the hot blood was gushing and about to burn out of her veins. Before losing her consciousness completely, she felt him over her and his hot breath burning her face. At last the Satan burst with roaring laughter overjoyed with his new victory.

She doesn't know how much time she remained in this state before she recovered her consciousness completely. Although she was conscious of a great deal of what had happened, her mind could not absorb completely what had exactly occurred. Her thoughts are disturbed and her head is still dizzy, Sheikh Ali still sitting on the carpet closing his eyes solemnly and the beads of the rosary still following each other in their monotonous movement she wore her clothes slowly and stood before him, her head bent low in shame. He said quietly:

- "The difficult stage has passed, Ahmed will marry you and you will beget boys and girls, soon you will see the result of what has happened just now, but you must come to me again ".

She left his house feeling as if her breath is going to be stifled her tear flowed copiously down her cheeks. She disliked going home directly. She preferred to go to Ahmed's home. She found his mother who received her eagerly and gladly saying:

- "Where have you been today?" I have been waiting a long time for you. At last I sent for you but your mother said that you went out without telling her where you going, where have you been?

- I have been to one of my friends. She sends for me for something important and urgent that was why I have forgotten to tell my mother.

- Come near me". Ahmeds mother made room for her it sit close to her, put her hand on her shoulder and asked her :

- "What do you think about Ahmed"?

Her eyes widened, and her heart trembled beating violently. She was stunned and found herself unable to reply. Ahmed's mother said simply. Smiling well – naturally;

- Ahmed wants to marry you and would like to know your opinion so as to go to your parents to betroth you, she suppressed a cry about to come out her lips then jumped and ran towards the door, before reaching it she turned back, bent kissing Ahmed's mother on her head, cheeks, hands, and every part of her body, then ran again to the door and went home. The news of Ahmed's proposal to marry her made her forget what had happened between her and Sheikh Ali and removed that grief and sorrow which perched on her soul.

[10]

The windows of hope and dreams are wide open before Ikhlas. Her family relatives and friends are making preparations for the wedding she has waited long to see this moment but what had happened in Sheik Ali's room is still troubling her mind. She wished if it has not happened. She tried to persuade herself that had to have happen or else how could she realize her dreams. There was no other alternative. But should she do? She must get ready to the grand night Ahmed must find her virgin otherwise everything she has been building all these years will collapse. The rescue came from one of her friends who advised her to go to a renowned surgeon famous for girls who sinned and omitted adultery before marriage the operation was perfect but the greedy doctor took a large sum of money from her.

Days passed quickly. The marriage was concluded but she never felt happy as she had been expecting while she was party listening to songs and watching people dancing cheerfully, she felt that there is something is missing... Something unknown to her. She spent several days at her home, as the custom, before leaving finally to her husband's home. During these few days she discovered that the man of whom she dreamt day and night, and for whom she wait so many years is far from her. She tried to be patient on the advice of Sheik Ali who told her that things need some time. It is true that everything in big house became at her call but the gap between Ahmed and herself is getting wider everyday although Shiek promised her that he will be as a ring in her finger or a toy in the hands of a child … He will certainly love her more than any husband can love his wife but she must be patient until the effect of magic is gone. But she is getting weary and afraid to lose self –control.

Her grudge and hatred for the women who stole Ahmed from her during her life and after her death multiplied.

Ahmed has got remoter and remoter from her life. He spends most of the day at work and never comes home before mid night. Even at weekends he brings Salma from his mother in law to spend the week end with his parents. He would then leave everything aside to respond to her demands, play and laugh with her. Ikhlas herself would press her depressor, suppress her hatred and do the same with Salma to please Ahmed. She would talk, play with her and carry her in her hands pretending that she loves her, while damning her in secret and wishing if she could struck her by the land and make her head break into pieces, never see her. Layla had die but it seems she had left her daughter and indignation.

She talked to Ahmed complaining that he hardly talks to her demanding him to give her more of his time expressing her disappoint and frustration. He promised her to be more attentive to her but he didn't keep his promise.

And now comes Salma's turn, which became her real headache and her major problem? What is the solution then? She added more water to the already wet clay.

Ahmed sees nothing than her in this world. She is his whole world. She must find a solution. She must find a way to keep Ahmed away from his daughter. But how? There is only one way, she must get a child. But how could she get a child while he is so distracted and indifferent to her. Ahmed renounces the whole world except that detestable girl, his daughter. She has to find some means. She has to go back to Sheik Ali. He is the only one who could solve this problem as he did before. He asked her to come back after marriage but she didn't go to him. The main reason of what she is now going through may be her long absence from him. That is why she must hasten to go to him before he gets angry and condemnations befall her.

She took the first opportunity and went to him. She knew very well the price she is going to pay but her malice, hatred and miserable condition in which she is living made her indifferent to anything that might happen to her. She came to him time and again. The dark brown tough hand continued to move feverishly up and down each inch of the soft worm body. .. The thick dry lips continued to swim freely on the breast and around the neck and recite charms between the well developed breast, and the long, thin, red tongue continued to rub the sensitive organs with purgatorial ointment. The Satan continued to be victorious, but now in her full consciousness. Awareness and consent. The bed became more preferable than the carpet. She had to find somebody to quench that fire. Her visits to Sheik Ali became more frequent. She is stuck fast and deep in the mine of sin. It is too late to pull out from it now. Sheik Ali asked her to bring one piece of her husband's underclothes, then give her something to mix with her husband's drink and something else to put under his mattress. He told her he will be fed up with his daughter, neglect her, and cease to love her as she used to do, His behavior as a husband will change within few days. As usual Sheik Ali's forecasts came to be true she soon felt a change in his behavior He became more aversive, closer quieter and more attached to the house suddenly her menstruation stopped she got panicked. Misgivings and forebodings attacked her violently.

The embryo in her womb does not belong to her husband but to sheik Ali. What shall she do? And how she is going to deal with it. How could she resort and whom could she trust? She perplexed. The world became dark in her sight. She thought about her mother. She is the only human being worthy of keeping her secret, enabling her to escape the scandal and assisting her to get rid of her disgrace before it is too late. But can tell her mother the fact? But how can she look in her eyes after that... No no she can't tell her mother she is pregnant by another man. There is no other person to resort to but Sheik Ali.

It is he who made her entangled in this disastrous situation for and he has to work out some solution for her distress. Tomorrow she will go to him. But suddenly an idea came to her mind like a flash of lightning. She sat straight in bed... why should she get rid of her fetus. Isn't she in bad need for a child to distract Ahmed from Salma and make him closer to her? What if she couldn't bring a child from Ahmed after getting rid of the fetus? How could she be sure of that? …. But what if her husband discovered that it doesn't belong to him but how can he discover that. Of he won't be able to know unless she volunteered by herself to tell him the truth. Sheik Ali and Ahmed have the same height but Sheikh Ali's nose is a bit flat, his hair is coarse and has a dark –brown. Complexion. But the colour of her complexion and the soft black hair will make the difference unnoticeable.

After all the child may come out like her of May, at least, take some of her features. Nobody than her can distinguish that Ahmed is not his father. That is her own secret and she must not divulge it to any other human being even Sheikh Ali should not know she is going to have a child from him. From now on she must stop her visits to him as long as nobody has yet discovered that she had been used to visit him.

Since she is going to have a child who shall uproot all her problems, there is no need to go to that small dark room any more. However, she remained for a long period indecisive about herself and avoid a probable scandal or let it grow without interfere convincing herself that is a gift sent to her by God to guarantee her husband's love for her. But time is running. People will soon know about her pregnancy. At last she decided to break the news for her husband as soon as possible. One day she combed her hair, put on her most beautiful dress and sprayed the sweetest perfume on her body and cloths. That days Ahmed came home very upset disturbed, sore, grieved and desperate. Although she made tremendous effort to know why he is so sad and hopeless, her attempts increased his annoyance and disturbance. But she must tell him now or else gloomy moments and the sad atmosphere which overshadowed the room, she broke the news. He stood still. She felt his annoyance and disturbance have multiplied.

(11)

A hmed had been occupying on important and sensitive job. He had acquired good experience in his field of work that he had been fond of and dedicated to. He has no political parties one deeply preoccupied in constant dissensions and conflicts to control power. He is not affiliated to any political party.

He has no enmity with decision makers. In his opinion allegiance should be to homeland, and the best service that the individual can offer for his people and nation is to try to perform his work as perfect as possible. He believed that agreement and progressing forward is better than disagreeing which always leads a deadlock. He has no grudge against anyone. Even his grief and sorrow for his wife were not able to make him hate those who had prevented him to take her abroad for treatment. He has heard numerous about the dismissal of some senior official by ruling regime for common good as they say but he had not the least doubt he will be one of them as his job is so sensitive and needs high efficiency and certain skills, but at the end of the one work day he received a letter exemption him from his job without mentioning to any reason or justification. At first he thought there must be some mistake which will be put right soon but several months passed without anything new.

Ikhlas gave birth to a boy similar to her in everything except the curly hair and the thick lips. She was disappointed. She wished if the newborn was a girl to replace Salma in Ahmed heart. Strangely enough Ahmed felt strange feeling towards the baby but blamed himself for this unordinary feeling. He knew it will add more to his family responsibilities. He must do something to support them. He must not continue to depend on his father. He waited for long expecting them to send for him to remedy his situation, repatriate work and apologize for their mistake. After the birth of new child he thought for a long time and found it is better for him to accept his father offer to work with him in his flourishing trade on condition that he is free to go back to his previous work if they discovered their mistake and sent for him. His father was very glad. At last his son agreed to join him he really needs assistance. He can no longer control his extensive trade and Ahmed is young, competent intelligent, honest credible and reliable. But from the first day in business, he felt as if he is a bird imprisoned in cage tightly shut. Is this logical? Is it fair to study all your life then at the end work in an occupation totally irrelevant to your studies, specialization on experience? Is it possible after all the efforts you made to contribute to the welfare of his country and people to be discharged in such way? To get rid of him at the summit of his is a loss for the country before being a loss of him. And why had they replaced him with a person who ignores the basic principles of the job? If the qualification of the person who replaced him are equivalent to, or better than his qualifications he would have felt less sorry. These thoughts remained revolving in his mind for a long while. All his life he was unable to assimilate why and how, many people pay homage for one person or one party and not for homeland.

Despite this bitter conflict inside him and despite his lack of belongingness to the sellers, goods and trade as a whole, he continued to go to the market until he became familiar to it. But days had been hiding something worse than all this for him. After a short period of his work in the market with his father, a new war broke out between ruling regime on the one hand and the merchants on the other hand.

Trade started to experience recession as a result of regulations set by the government whose main goal is to expel original merchants from the market as a preliminary step to control it as it did with all other government institutions. The pressure began with imposing additional fees on commodities and services higher than the original prices to create a state of confusion, chaos and instability to give way direct intervention by some monitoring and security quarters.

Prices escalated crazily. Most people were unable to purchase their basic life necessities. It became almost impossible for them to obtain their daily bread. The government imposed custody on bakeries and started to distribute bread among diabetics and other patient through its institutions one or two loaves per day. Bread came to be disposed of the same as medicine, bodies became thin and emaciated, bones projected and eyes bulged. Many villages and cities became like ghosts cities which people see in unreal films, children lost their innocence. They came to live permanently in the street. Some of them became cart drivers or shoe polishers to help their families, other became thieves and beggar and all of them became addicts by smelling benzene and other dangerous materials to forget their pains and miserable conditions. The ruling authority continued to put obstacles on the way of merchants arresting and imprisoning large numbers of them, in an unprecedented case the criminal count corrected a young merchant to death when the secret police found with him few banknotes of foreign currency whose transaction was prohibited by the government. The case engaged public opinion long time. All people thought the punishment shall either be the confiscation of the money or imprisonment for six or seven months as maximum in the case was so trifle but the penalty was unbelievable. Before the execution of the sentence, the merchant's mother who was scared, kept running from government official to another beseeching them to intercede to alleviate the horrible sentence of her only son but they all kept silent as if they were dead and their hearts are made of rock.

She offered to give them all her and her family wealth, houses, cars, any things concern them to ease the punishment but they were refused. They wanted to send a message to all merchants that death shall be the destiny of whoever of them violates their unjust laws. The young merchant was hanged so as to be an example to anyone who does not submit to their will or challenge their power.

After her son's execution, the wretch mother lost her mind and went wondering aimlessly from street to street. After the sorrowful end of the young merchant and his mother, a large number of merchants hastened to liquidate their business and leave the country without return. Before that many of them declared their bankrupt due to the exorbitant taxes levied by the government. Ahmed's father was determined to continue on his business despite the pressure. He believes it is his duty in theses harsh conditions to make consumer goods available to poor people at affordable prices. Therefore he collected all his money plus additional funds from his friends as credits and hired five ships and send them to load with basic consumer goods although his close friends warned him not to put all his eggs in one basket He knew these goods might expose him to great risks but he didn't care as his first and foremost concern is to extend a helping hand to the poor and hungry people. The ships anchored at the port but the authorities issued an urgent order to confiscate all their contents with the pretext of import prohibition although the import license was issued before the order but by hook or crook they wanted to destroy honest merchant.

Ahmed and his father tried, in vain to release the cargo. They appointed a lawyer but the case was defending repeatedly until they became desperate. For the second time Ahmed feel angry as he never felt before. On what grounds were these goods confiscated? Why should the government give his aged father such a hard blow?

Changes came rapidly and successively and misfortunes be fell Ahmed's Family one after other. Under all these hard circumstances Ahmed found himself faced with the responsibilities of supporting his family in addition to his parents. He was not worried about his small family but he was anxious about his parents who were used to standard of living whom he can't provide. Moreover, Ahmed knows very well his father's self pride. Therefore he felt a pressing need to find work... Any work to make his father avoid humiliation of bankrupt. He practiced several marginal activities and at last settled mini bus driver, goes to work at dawn and comes back home about midnight exhaust and weary with the loud voices of sellers and shouts of commissioners buzzing in his years and the voice of the minibus stations echoing in his ears even while he is sleeping. His visits to Salma got lesser and lesser until they are about to stop completely.

[12]

Two years had passes since the small family left the old residential quarter and moved to another one. Life became gloomier and monotonous sine they hired that small ugly house which is typical to Ikhlas house in the old residential quarter. All her dreams had slipped, evaporated and gone with the wind... Her husband's high ranking in civil service ... Her father in law huge fortune ... luxury life .... The big house which she had dreamt long years to become its crowned queen, now she is so sad and sorry to lose forever. Her gloom has multiplied as her husband continued to remain away from home most of the time. Although the idea of conception for the second time never departed from her mind. Since she touched his aversion and indifference about the first child. She became possessed the idea of bringing another child especially during the last days. She thought her husband- the remaining dream of her dreams – does not spend all his time at work as he told her but with his daughter at her grandmother's home leaving her ruminating her sadness and pains alone, waiting for him hour after hour to come back home. One day sat thinking why couldn't she get pregnant from Ahmed until now although both of them have no physical defect. She is a mother and Ahmed is a father. Is it because they meet as strangers? Is it because he has no interest or desire to have a child from her? Or is it because she felt, through all these years, he is so remote and alien to her despite their co- existence in the same house. She is eager to be getting a girl, what should she do? Should she go back to sheikh Ali? But this will involve great risk. He might discover her secrete with supernatural power. No, No she has to find a safer way. Her Imagination drifted away to her feverish encounters with Sheikh Ali in the small dark room and the ecstasy of the last moment between consciousness and unconsciousness. She felt her blood circulation accelerating. While she was deeply absorbed in her thought and memories with Sheikh Ali. She was interrupted by knocks on the outer door. She ran quickly and opened it. The knocker was Ali, her neighbors' son. He came to tell her that his mother and her neighbors are waiting for her to drink coffee with them as usual. Ali used to come to her house at anytime. His mother used to send him to give something to her or borrow something from her. She depends on him to do many things for her. Sending him to market to bring something for her, paint a table, or repair the door lock... etc. He is free to enter or exit from the house at any time. She is used to him coming and going out of her house several times a day. His presence did not excite a feeling in her in the past but this time she found herself looking at him fixedly as if she sees him for the first time. He has just passed the adolescence. His mouth ache has grown thinly, his nose is erect like a sword and his shoulder became broad. Suddenly she was possessed by an unruly desire to embrace him... an uncontrolled desire that nearly stifled her breath. She quickly invited him to come in to give him something to deliver to his mother. When she entered she closed the door and walked behind him devouring him with her looks. In fact she was lying. She has nothing to send to his mother but she felt a compelling emotion to keep him with her as long as possible. He became aware of her strange perplexing looks and hastened to ask her to give him the thing she wanted to give to his mother she opened the kitchen cupboard, put some coffee powder in a small glass bottle and put it in his hand trembling as a result of excessive emotion He took the bottle and hurried away not understanding why has she been behaving like this. When Ali left the house she dropped in her bed shaking like a small sparrow swept away by s violent snow storm. After sometime she was able to control herself. When she went for coffee she found herself undesired to sit and talk as usual with her friends. She pretended to go to the latrine twice hoping to see Ali anywhere in the house. She was captured by an unknown evil feeling towards that decent and innocent boy as a butterfly is drawn to a glazing light in a 0 dark night.

Ikhlas remained for several days trying to resist a mad desire for Ali like a hungry lions afraid to lose her mind if she kept resisting like this. She couldn't sleep his image always in her eyes. Occupying her thoughts every minute. Even at the coffee gathering every day, she feels bored and unable to concentrate on their conversation as if their voices come from another world too far away from her. Sometimes she holds the coffee cup for a long time forgetting that it is in her hands until the coffee becomes cold. Other times she would raise the cup to her mouth and out of it in a monotonous mechanical movement unaware whether it is full or empty. She always finds herself involuntarily concentrating on Ali's movement in the house. She know whether he went from this to that room, opened the water cooler or watching the television. If he happiness to pass near the coffee gathering for any reason, her mad desire to embrace him to her breast with all her burning passion attacks her violently, and when she feels she is about to lose self – control, she hastens to leave her place with any pretext. Hurries for home, enter her room, and throw herself in bed shaking with passion, turning hysterically from side to side in bed until she comes to herself and gets calm.

One day she left the coffee assembly somewhat earlier telling her friends that one of the electric lamps in the house needs replacement with a new one, she will need Ali to do the task. She went to his room and asked him to join her at home to take out the dies functioning lamp ad fix the new one, then left quickly for her house. In the morning, before she came to the coffee assembly she deliberately replaced the good lamp in her room with a bad one to bring Ali to her bedroom. When she arrived, she quickly undressed and put o a short red transparent silk sleeping shirt open at the breast and without sleeves. When Ali knocked the outer door she opened it then closed it behind him and started to walk in front of him swaying in coquetry dalliance. This was the first time for Ali to see her in such an amazing fascinating appearance. He felt dryness in his tongue and scorching heat in his throat. She entered the dark room and invited him to come in. He came after her in fear and confusion mixed with awes. She planned to test his reaction before doing something rash and spoil everything. Before going to the coffee gathering she closed the windows to blur his eyes and prevent him from seeing clearly. She intentionally stood on his way to touch her body when he passes. When his shoulder collided with her breast she moaned and groaned in coyness a sweet voice. She felt his tension and noticed his breathlessness. She knew they share the same thoughts. Suddenly that irresistible desire attacks her violently. She was no longer able to be cautions. She forgot her plan of dragging him gradually, bit by bit. His eyes were not yet accustomed to the faint light of the room when he felt her arms around his body pressing him tightly to her. He felt a sudden fear but the smell of her hot breath licking his face, lips and nose as a hunger wild cat licks a bowel full of pure milk, he forgot his fear. The house was empty. She moaning and hissing like snake, then started to shout wildly. He was panicked. He hastened to put the pillow on her mouth nearly stifling her breath. At last she became clam and silent as if her soul departed from her body.

He put on his clothes and stool looking at her. She was lying on her back, her hands on her breast?? Her eyes closed. She was very quiescent. He thought she was dead He became more scared but he waited for a while not knowing what to do. At last he saw her chest rising and descending regularly and slowly. He hastened to leave the house feeling ashamed and disgraced. He felt as though he had been in a horrible nightmare.

This was the first time for him to touch a woman. He entered his room, closed the door, threw himself on his bed and cried for a long time feeling God will never forgive him and the door of hill will be wide open to devour his body in the Day of Judgment.

Ikhlas remained on bed for a long time, calm and happy for the first time since marriage. She came to herself gradually and smiled amusing... Now she can bring a girl easily. From now on Ali will be at her disposal whenever she wants him to come, and she, on her side, will never stop calling him unless she is sure she became pregnant and no longer needs him. It is true he will repent for a day or two because he will think he could do so but when the desire burn inside him he will come and throw himself cryingly petitioningly in her breast and begging her, he drunk from the salty water after along thirst and he couldn't stop because that water is just increased his thirst day after day and there is no way infront of him except to come back to her to quench his thirst and to satisfy his desire, she must get pregnant to revenge from Layla and Salma and Ali is her only means to realize this dream she has no intention to go to Sheikh Ali and Ahmed does not even feel she existing. She is expecting the girl she will bring will be prettier than Salma because Ali is a handsome boy and has the same complexion and soft hair as her. She will capture Ahmed's heart and take Asma's place.

As she expected, Ali became at her beck and call whenever she wants him. Not only that but he became careful to stay with her as long as she wants him to stay. Despite the pain and feeling of quilt which trouble his mind after coming out of her house, despite the contradictory sinful life he is leading with Ikhlas in secret and what he does in public his constant attendance of the five daily prayers at the mosque and religious lessons held every Monday and Thursday, despite his extreme fear from God, he was quite helpless to became jumbled, messy and mixed up, the colour of his complexion got dark and his face turned pale. His mother was alarmed to see him like this but she couldn't know what was happening to him. When Ikhlas felt the embryo moving in her womb and observed the anxiety of Ali's mother, she decided to get rid of him before his mother discovers the secret relation between her and her son. To her, what is occurring between her and Ali is transient whim which possessed her for some time. The quailed down and disappeared like a sudden fit of fever. She wanted to have a child and now the fetus is moving in her womb. She must stop this dangerous adventure forever and immediately before it is too late. But Ali couldn't leave her. His attachment to her is stronger than anything. When she asked him not to come again, he cried for a long time and beseeched her not to abandon him because he can't leave her. He is really mad of her. Many times he comes without being called to satiate his flaming desire at any place in the house, her bed room, kitchen or even the bathroom. She tried many times to make him understand that his mother beginning to suspect and may soon discover what is going on between them but he was deaf and blind unable to hear or seen anything. She became really afraid of his rashness. She threatened him if he does not stop his irrational behavior, she will be forced to tell his mother that he tried to rape her. When she told him this, he felt deeply injured. He thought she loves him as he loves her. He couldn't imagine accept idea that she no longer wants him. He believed that she maybe fell in love with another person; He felt doubt and jealousy eating him. He could neither sleep nor eat. He started to watch the door of her house day and night to see the person he thought he replaced him in her heart. She became really worried of his unreasonable behavior. But she was, at last relieved when he was admitted to the university and went away to stay at the students hotel. All her attention became focused on her pregnancy. She started to count the days hoping to bring beautiful girl.

The months of pregnancy passed and Ikhlas gave birth to a boy apposite, as usual, to all her hopes. And expectations. The boy came out typically to her. For the second time she notices Ahmed's aversion from the baby. She was really amazed from Ahmed's indifference about the child. All year passed since the birth of the child she felt bored, depressed and miserable again. She longed for Ali and wished if he is her now. Therefore, she decided to trap another boy to substitute him. She was able to hunt another boy and spent a few weeks with hum, then shifted to another and another ... However, she was very careful not to get pregnant. She developed the habit of using excessive cosmetic to attract the attention of her preys. To keep away from the danger of being suspected or discover she started to select boys from other residential quarters.

(13)

Salma didn't feel lonely since she started to live with her grandmother permanently she felt the need for her mother and her father. It is true she missed their presence in her life but she never felt lonely. Her grandmother encompassed her with love, kindness, sympathy, compassion, and tenderness. She saw in Salma her beloved departing daughter. Salma exchanged the same feeling and emotion with her dear grandmother. During the first days after her mother's death Salma was dismayed, panicked, scared, alarmed and horrified. She was crying all time. She wanted all people calling for her mother and crying bitterly. However, the presence of her father and grandmother beside her all the time alleviated the shock of her mother's loss, with the lapse of days and months, the repeated question about whereabouts of her mother lessened.

The dedicated care of her father had great effect in compensating her for the loss of her dear mother. She became used to wait impatiently for his return from work in the evening the happiest moments of her day when he arrives carry a toy, some sweets or some new cloths for her. He used to stay with her playing and laughing together? She falls asleep. But when the intervals between his visits elongated as a result of his constant preoccupation after dismissal from his work, confiscation of his father's cargo and his perpetual attempts to provide the minimum limit of the basic necessities for his parents and small family, Salma's life became empty once more. She again restarted asking about her mother, the first days of disruption of her father visits she insisted to sit in front of their outer door waiting for him to come. When the time passes and she gets bored desperate and tired of waiting she usually comes back to her grandmother and asks her.

- "When will mother come back?"
- Her grandmother would embrace her tenderly while her tears flow on her cheeks and then would answer her:
- "when she finishes her studies."
  Salma would ask again:
- "And when will her studies finish?"
- "Soon baby, soon"

Salma would go to sleep so sad clinging to the hope that her father or mother will come tomorrow.

She was admitted to the elementary school where she found some consolation in the illustrated books with their beautiful colours especially the coloured pictures of animals. Although her father was too preoccupied, Salma excelled her school mates. She was able to capture the hearts of her teachers with innocent beauty, decent character, good nature, excellent behavior and easy- going nature years passed. She was very happy with her school. At the end of the elementary stage, she sat for the intermediate stage examination very sure that she is going to get high marks. As all expected she was the top of the distinct at which she sat for the examination. Her grandmother was very happy. She made a big party to celebrate the occasion where she invite Salma's teachers and school mates, her grandparents, all her maternal and paternal relatives and neighbors'. That was a grand day in Salma's life had it not been for the absence of her mother and father because the minibus in which he works as driver need repair. He had to miss the party to go to the mechanic. She felt her father failed her although he came the next day and stay with her for a long time, For not being able to come, She was not able to forget that he is the only person who does not attend her party. His indifference about her is unforgiveable although he did his best to explain to her that he was forced not attend the party.

The summer school holiday was about to end in the midst of her happiness with her success but a few weeks to the end of the holiday, her grandmother who is a diabetic for the last twenty years, had to stay in bed due to the complication of diabetes. Salma looked after her, her health has improved and started to move here and there in the house. Salma was very happy. She thought that her grandmother is on her way to recovery but suddenly, diabetes paroxysm attacked her and died smiling contently as if she is happy to join to her daughter. Salma wept bitterly feeling for the second time she is at a loss and as lonely as nobody else in this desolate.

(14)

On the third day of the death of Salma's grandmother Ahmed was sitting near his father who asked him:

- "What are you going to do?"
  Ahmed said: "with regards to what"
- "With regards to Salma... She is now young girl passing through an important stage of her life and needs to be close to you more than any time."
- Ahmed bowed his head for a while and Said
- "Yes father, you are right. I will take her to live with me".

Ahmed had thought about Salma since the death of her grandmother but had not decided with whom she should stay. The short dialogue with his father decided the matter and left no other options to him.

The funeral days passed and Salma left the residential quarter in which she spent her childhood and the house in which she spent her most memorable part of her life. She moved to another distant residential quarter and a new house where she felt from the first moments she is unwelcomed and unwanted.

The summer holiday came to an end. Salma's father enrolled her at school in a neighboring residential quarter. When Ikhlas knew, she became very upset protesting that the school needs fees, books, new school uniform and other expenses and Ahmed's resources are too meager. Is it not enough that she will eat and sleep? Is it not enough that he brought her to spoil her life? Is it not enough that Ahmed spends most of his income on his parents? She tried with her wickedness and cunning to change Ahmed's mind that the best thing for Salma is to stay at home. She is now grown up girl and should marry as soon as possible. There is no need for school. Marriage is better when Ahmed disregarded her opinions, she became more upset. And decided not to let Salma's live peacefully or succeed in school. She swore to make Salm's life like hell and give her no opportunity to concentrate on her study. Since Ahmed spends most of the day away from home Ikhlas found ample time to harass Salma who never told her father or complain to him.

Instead, she endured all kind of molestation from her step mother and the two brothers. The more the harassment of Ikhlas and her two brother increases, the more Salm'a endurance becomes stronger. Salma's sadness was increasing day after day due to the cruelty of her step mother, the bad treatment she received from her, the unceasing attempts to make her life like hell while her father was not aware of Salma's situation. On the other hand she knew her father had enough problems and little time to care for her. She neither considers him blamable nor does she want to add more to his troubles. Therefore she decided to keep her own troubles and problems to herself, determined not to disturb him although she is in bad need for his love, care and affection. Only one person felt that need from the first look. That person was Osman son of a rich man called Mansour who lives in the neighboring aristocratic residential quarter. When Salma came to live with her father, Osman had been absent, sent by his father to study in a foreign country after he had failed in his study or work in his country. He spent two years abroad. After two days of his return he went to Omer's grocery near Salma's home to buy some cigarettes' and greet Omer who was used to sit with him for hours and hours in front of the grocery before her travelled abroad. He was longing to see his friend and know what had happened during his absence. Just at that time Salma was leaving the grocery. Osman saw her carrying some pieces of soap to wash a heap of clothes collected by Iklas to be washed by Salma to preoccupy her as much as possible from memorizing her lessons. Osman saw her fascinating beauty and the heavy deep sadness in her charming eyes. He stood looking at her quite stared and followed her with his look until she opened the door of the house and entered, then he went to meet Omer. His heart was full of joy.

Osman was brought up in middle class family. He was very spoilt as he was the only boy among four girls.

When the military coup took power, Osman's father, who had been a minor employee in a local bank, joined it, and hence the doors of wealth opened before him. Within a few years he became one of the richest people in the country. His extensive business and the numerous tasks charged to him by the party distracted him from looking after his family. He left all family affairs including supervision of their children to his wife who took the opportunity to spend extravagantly specially on her children, particularly Osman. Anything he wants will bring for him whatever it might cost.

The result was complete failure at school. To spend his leisure time, He joined a corrupted clique composed of a number of boys belonging, like him, to wealthy families, leading a dissolute life, spending most of their time loitering in the streets, laughing loosely and molesting school girls.

Since Osman was afraid to be discovered by his father, he smoked secretly. But his friends tempted him to drink wine. Osman did not like its taste.

He swore not to taste it all his life. Unlike his friends, Osman was not satisfied with flirtation and harassment of girls. He wanted to extinguish that unruly desire inside him and discharge that excessive energy which found no body to guide and direct towards proper channel.

Therefore, he went further than his peers and started to spend his leisure time in love advantages, illicit sexual relations and chasing university girls and civil service employees.

The deteriorating economic conditions of the country were an opportune atmosphere for practicing debauchery. Most families become poor including the middle class which in the past had led decent and dignified life. Need forced many girls to fall prey to Osman and his likes. The noble principles preserved the community's morals had disappeared and replaced by degeneration of moral values and corruption of all sorts and forms. Osman was completely absolved in illicit relations.

He acquired vast experience in dealing with women. He knows very well how to handle theme. It is seldom that women could escape from his clutch like a spider from which poor flies rarely escape from its wet. The more they try to escape, the more they find theme selves entrapped, helpless and finally resign to their inevitable destiny. His tools in tempting women, his luxuriant car, expensive dresses, Parisian perfume and above all his dexterity and ability to act any role dictated by the situation. His reputation as women trapper reached his father who was, at that time, nominated occupy a high vacant political post. Since he was afraid to lose this golden opportunity because of his son's behavior, he decided to send him abroad to study computer since or any specialty else as he might commit a shameful act and spoil his father's political future. Then he quickly made the necessary arrangements for his son's departure to get rid of him and to give him an opportunity to learn something that might make him a self dependent person instead of loitering in the streets and chasing women.

Osman was very glad. He saw in travelling abroad a new kind of amusing adventure which would give him a chance to meet new kind of women. Once he arrived, he plunged himself into endless sexual relations, dancing halls and casinos wasting all the money sent to him secretly by his mother. His father was appointed in the eminent political position. A friend of his father met him, when he was there for business, and telephoned Osman's father to give him an idea about how his son was behaving there. The father's friend told him that his son deserted his study from the first month and started from that time until now to lead a life of debauchery. His father got very upset and ordered him to come back immediately. He told his wife not to send him money anymore and swear to divorce her if she did so. When he came back, his father reprimanded him toughly but he received his reproach coldly and apathetically. When he finished the last cigarette in his pocket, he went out to buy a new cigarette box from the grocery of his friend Omer. It is just at that time he saw Salma for the first time. He asked Omer, as he was known for his talkativeness, fondness of following up the news of other people and backbiting and calumny, to tell him about Salma. He told him all he knew about her and concluded at the end of his report that she is a polite girl. Her only movement is from home to school and vice versa. She comes to the grocery sometimes to buy what she needs quietly and politely. Finally, he said with laughing she is not the type of girl that interest you. Osman smiled cunningly because Omer dose not know that Salma is specifically the type of women he likes best, search for and rarely finds. A kind of challenge more tempting than (easy to obtain) women. Salma was very confused to see the penetrating searching look of Osman. Their eyes met for a moment while she was leaving the grocery. That confusion ravished suddenly once she arrived home and became engrossed in washing, ironing and cleaning. Next morning when she was going to school she saw him leaning on the street lamp post fixing his eyes on their door as if he was waiting for some specific person to come out.

Last day Salma was not sure about the features of his face but this morning, despite the long distance between them she was able to distinguish that penetrating searching look. She felt the same confusion as yesterday. She closed the door behind her and walked quickly away at a distance from the light post and continued to walk with her eyes fixed to the ground. When she turned to the next street, she felt some comfort and quietude. The school day ended. She came back, as usual, on foot feeling exhausted and thirsty due to the scorching heat and the long distance from the school to the house but when she turned to the street leading to the house she saw him standing leaning on the light post looking towards the direction from which she was coming. Their eyes met for a while for the second time this day. She forget her thirst and weariness and walked quickly, about to run, towards the house. Unusually she knocked on the door repeatedly and continuously. At last the door was opened. She entered hurriedly and closed it behind her feeling anxious, scared and disturbed.

After she entered, a smile was drawn on Osman's face. He left the place feeling satisfaction and contentment. He noticed her haste and confusion when she saw him and understood why she was trying to keep at a distance from where he was standing. This indicates he was successful in attracting her attention and this was more than he had been expecting so far and more than what he had been hoping for.

Osman continued his habit of standing at the light post which became something quite familiar to Salma who tried, at the beginning, to ignore his looks wherever she opens the door or passes by him. But his looks have changed from the penetrating and scrutinizing looks to tender and beseeching looks and she started to ask herself what does he want from me? Why dose he come at such an early hour and stand alone waiting for her to pass by him? What are these strange looks? Dose he remain standing like this all the day or he comes and goes and then comes back. Dose he wait for another girl and she is just imagining he waits for her? But if he waits for another girl why dose he follows her with his eyes whenever she comes or goes? No, I feel he waits for me specifically and not for any other girl. But why did not he talk to her until now? Why did not he do anything to indicate that he comes especially for her? Perhaps he is waiting for an opportunity to talk to her. In spite of his daring looks, will he have the courage to do that? And what could he say to her? Dose she have the courage to exchange talk with him. These and many other questions kept revolving in her mind insistently. Although she found no answering for them but she began to give more attention to her appearance and stand for a long time in front of the mirror on the morning before going to school. Once she steps out of the door, she sees him and her eyes meet his eyes and her heart beats violently. The pulses of her heart accelerate when she gets near the place where he stands. When she passes him, and before turning to the other street she usually feels a strong desire to turn her head to see is he still following her with his eyes.

She finds great difficultly to resist this persistent desire but finds herself able to restrain it. But Osman kept waiting patiently confident that this moment is imminent. She will turn her head soon. Only at this moment he will be able to commence the second part of his plan. Only he had to wait and not for long this time.

15

One Thursday morning Salma woke up early to meet her father before he leaves for work to ask him to let her to spend the weekend with her grandparents.

She is sure he would agree but her main motive is to take the transport fare from him to go to the house of the grandparents. IKhlas exhausted her with continuous hard work all week. Although she woke up early but her father left for work a bit earlier more than usual that day. Her longing for her grandparents was not the only reason for going to them.

In addition to that, she wanted to escape from the drudgery and her everyday routine and give her tired body some rest.

As usual IKhlas annoyed her with her injurious insults. She left home without drinking her morning tea feeling she is in need to talk to anybody. She found Osman standing as usual. Her eyes met his eyes . . . this time the tender beseeching look touched something inside her. She passed by him as she used to do every day but when she arrived to the end of the street, she could not resist her desire to turn her head. . . their eyes met. . . he smiled tenderly to her. . . she quickly turned to the other street and continued on her way. She was no more upset or gloomy. Osman left his place with feeling of a hunter who is about to entrap his prey. Today she took her first step towards him and she will never be able to return. He is now sure he can continue his plan exactly as he designed; no more no less.

Salma become used to the tender looks of Osman which she used to exchange with embraced looks. She no longer resists her desire to turn her head when she reaches the end of the street on the morning and when she comes back from the school in the afternoon to see his nice smile. She often goes to the bathroom, and climbs on the small iron seat and look at Osman through the window of the bathroom. Osman took another step .He become used to wave his hand to her before she enters the house when there is no people. She feels great happiness.

At last she found somebody who pays attention, greet, smile and stand all the day to see her and wave his hand to her. This satisfied her vanguard touched her deeply. Osman has become spiritual nourishment for her soul; his image is constantly in her eyes and mind. One morning she stood before the mirror after putting on her clothes which she washed and ironed for a long time. She turned around to have a last look at her dress on which she extended a big effort to appear as beautiful as possible. Although the dress dose not appear as she wanted, she felt quite satisfied when she looked attentively at her charming face and combed her black soft hair.

When she was quite sure that everything is all right, she went out hastily hopping Osman might see her in her fascinating appearance. She was confident that she will find him standing waiting for her, but she found the outer courtyard quite empty. She turned her head left and right excepting to see him somewhere, but there was no trace for him.

She was very disappointed. She walked slowly deliberately hoping he will appear at any moment thinking that something might have delayed him. But when she reached the end of the street and turned to the other street she became desperate. She arrived at school very upset. She felt there is something important missing. She sat in her class annoyed and tensioned feeling the school day will never end.

When she heard the bell ringing ending the school day, she sighed deeply and hastened to leave the school as if she was leaving a prison in which she remained for long years. She crossed the distance to the street leading to the courtyard, where Osman was used to stand, in a short time, and turned to the street which leads to her house. She was shocked for the second time, to see the place empty as she left it on the morning except from a woman carrying a bundle of firewood over her head, tying a child around her back, holding an axe under her armpit and a basket of food leftover with one hand.

Salma's feeling of frustration increased. She slowed down her steps to the maximum possible limit turning her head left and right expecting that he may be appear in any moment but he is not appear. She spent the rest of the day upset and depressed.

She spent all that night sleepless. Next morning, she left the house early but for the third day she finds no one on the street. She felt as if the street was laughing at her.

She was about to weep. The school day came to an end. Black thoughts and frustration engulfed her. It seems that she had been wrong; she thought stupidly she had meant something important to Osman. It seems he dose not bother about her, she interpreted his looks as she wished herself. He never talked to her nor did anything that makes her interpret his looks in the way she did. A wave of doubt overshadowed her and made her disbelieve everything and think she was imagining things. She even denied his signs and his hand with which he used to greet her and attributed this to delusions and to her desire to be close to any person who ever he is. She was walking towards her house feeling desperate dragging her legs. Opposite to her expectations she saw him standing at the same place as he always used to do. Her heart nearly jumped out from her chest. She became breathless, and blood gushed in her eyes.

She quickly passed by him and reached the door in moments but before knocking the door she turned her head. Their eyes met. He was smiling. He waved his hand. He was very elegant, his soft hair was combed. His tender look followed her and there was a nice look on his handsome face. She entered the house very happy and contented and spent the night on rose dreams. Next morning, she passed by him and looked directly in his face. She saw his lips whispering some words she could not identify those words but she was very happy. Yesterday he smiled as to apologize to her, this day he whispered to her. .

He really cares for her and comes specially to see her and nobody else. The school day ended and she left school eager to see him in the same place, but a few steps from the school she saw him suddenly in front of her and blocking her way. She was stunned. She was not expecting him to be so daring to come to school. Although she had prepared many scenarios in her mind if he talks or tries to talk to her, she stood frozen when he greeted her in melodious voice. She was not able to exchange his greeting. He stood looking at her for a while with a sweet smile filling his face. He took out a small orange envelope from his pocket and handed it to her. She tried to refuse but she saw a strange determination in his eyes. He said:

- "It is just a paper and will not cost you any things if you read it and if you do not like its contents tear it off pieces. I will not intercept your way again". She knows he will not leave before she takes the envelope. She was afraid he may go on his stubbornness and one of her teachers or one of her schoolmates sees her take the envelope.

She found the best thing to avoid an inevitable scandal is to take the message and let him leave her alone. She turned her head left and right cautious and afraid, then quickly snatched the envelope and threw it in her school bag and hurried away.

She felt the distance to the house very long and the time she waited for her stepmother to open the door as years. At last she was alone in her room. She took out the massage before taking off her school uniform. She opened it while her school bag was still hanging on her shoulder. The massage was crowded with sweet expressions of love and flirtation (I confide my love for you to the stars of heavens), (Seeing you become the only nourishment of my dreary life), (You angelic image never depart from me a sleep or awake).

While reading the message, Salma felt hovering in heaven of ecstasy and contentment.

She is thirsty for such sweet words. She felt the warm expressions intoxicate her. Dose that stranger love her to this extent? She read it many times and every time it makes better effects on her. When she went to sleep she put it under her pillow to touch it from time to time. For the first time She felt very happy and that night her dream are son nice and beautiful

Osman's message continued. Their nice expression and sweet words become which spiritual nourish which made her forget pains, aches and misery his message become the beautiful word to which she resort to compensate for her father's negligence, Ikhlas haltered and mistreatment and the harassment of her children. All her life was confined to Osman. She exchanged messages with him. He became indispensable to her to see. One day he waited for her on the way to school and requested from her to see him after the end of the school day at one of the near public parks to talk with her, listen to her voice and look in to her beautiful eyes. She sat absent minded in her class thinking about meetings him. At noon she hurried to the place he described to her in eager and mixed feelings.

16

The public park described by Osman was a busy place when neighboring families used to visit it, spend time and entertain themselves but during the last few years it became deserted place and only visited by street children to spend the night away from the eyes of the police, or passers-by to rest for a while and then leave it or stray dogs looking for shelter. It was not far from the school. She arrived within ten minutes and found Osman waiting for her, sitting on a wooden bench under a shady tree at the end of the park. Osman chose that place purposely for two reasons. The bench was not long enough to accommodate more than two persons and the tree hided the bench completely from other parts of the park. When he noticed she was hesitant and confused he pacified her with encouraging soothing words with well selected flirtation expressions until she becomes pacified, her fear and confusion were dispelled.

She wished if he would not stop for ever. He took this opportunity, drew her right hand, placed it between his hands and started to press it gently while continuing his sweet words.

A pleasant sensation infiltrated to her body for a while, and then she withdrew her hand quickly when she saw a person from the distance. She became confused once again, stood up immediately and requested to leave the park. He had expected she is going to spend longer time. He did not object so as not to appear impolite in their first meeting. She promised to meet him tomorrow at the same place. When they went out of the park her conscience reproached her severely. She felt as she committed a sin and asked God to forgive her and swore not to repeat what happened today in the park. But in spite of that she met

Osman again in the same place the next day, and she could not prevent
him from putting her hand between his hands as he did yesterday. She
allowed him to press her hand, play with her fingers and excited her
with a delightful sensation to which she submitted and was unable to
talk. That park became their preferred place where they meet every
afternoon, Osman uttering his sweet tender words and she listening as
if she was hypnotized forgetting her suffering and pains at home. She
became used to let her hand in his hands to play with it and press it as
long as he likes. One day he suggested they should change their meeting
place with the pretext that they remained meeting in this park for a long
time and it is better to go to another place otherwise they may attract
inquisition of people.

She asked him:

- "But when can we meet? "

- "We must meet in another more safe. A place further away than this
  park. I know a safe place about twenty minutes from here by car . . .
  it is nice, cozy and quite place where nobody knows us.

As usual he is proceeding according to a predesigned plan. During
this time he tried to convince her with the idea of going to the new place
by his car. Despite she refused to get in his car in a precedent time when
he offered to take her by his car from her home to school and vice versa.
He wanted to break this barrier. Salma became familiar with the park,
and thinks then there is no justification for changing it, she said:

- "But I cannot go with you in your car"

- The place is far away and will take more than an hour's on foot. The
  car is the only means that will enable us to go and come back in a
  reasonable time . . . I cannot understand why you refuse to come
  with me in the car?" "Are you afraid of me?"

- "I am not afraid of you, I am afraid of people" If changing the place
  is so necessary; let us look for place more nearly. As for the car, you
  know I cannot absolutely ride it.

- No Salma, you are not afraid of people or else because you are continue to meet me in this park every day. The truth is you are afraid to be alone with me even inside my car . . . I thought you loved me as I loved you and trusted me as I trusted you und you utterly believed it is impossible for me to do you any harm or hurt you, but it seems that I was mistaken . . . you neither love me salma, nor trust me but you are afraid of me. He dropped some tears from his eyes as he used to do in such situations, then stood up muttering.

- "I am sorry, from now on, I will never bother you. Then he stood up and hurried away.

She felt something heavy pressing her heart. She was affected by words. She saw tears dropping from his eyes and the sadness which over shadowed his face and thought she caused him great pain.

She had tried hardly to control herself and say something before he leaves but she could not say anything . . . her tongue was dumb and her brain was paralyzed. She could not utter a single word. She remained standing as if frozen following him with her eyes until he disappeared.

She did not know how she left the park, how she arrived home or how the door was opened, she was unaware of long time she remained standing in front of the door. She did not see lkhals looking at her in rejoicing when she saw her so sad and absent minded . . . she was neither affected by her sarcastic words nor her impudent laugh. She had reached the maximum level of pain and sadness. Her heart was filled with fear to lose Osman who became the pivot of her life. She was certain her existence and happiness are linked his existence. He is the oasis which shades her in the midst of the hell, deprivation, solitude, loneliness and isolation in which she lives. She sacrifices him if she had to sacrifice the whole world.

She cannot imagine that she is not going listen to his melodious voice and his sweet soft words. She remained for the rest of the day blaming and reproaching herself . . . She felt she had been unjust with him. What will happen if she rode the car with him? What is wrong if she met him anywhere? Talked together and spend a pleasant time . . . Nobody will know, who cares about her expect him? Since she came to live with him, her father was never aware where she goes when dose she come back. Her stepmother is usually at summit of her pleasure and happiness when Salma is outdoors, and her two sons do nothing but annoying and disturbing her. Nobody would bother to ask about her if she is absent. Nobody will miss her if she is late. He is the only one who asks about her. He is the only one who misses here. He is the only one who encompasses her with love, kindness, and sympathy. Why should she make him angry? Why should not respond to his request as long as he did not request something bad or evil? Dose not he deserve to given the same concern he gives to her? Dose not he spend the long rights to express his love and suffering in his massage? Has not he the right request to sit with her where he feels comfortable away from inquisitive eye? Yes he does deserve to give him some of her time, and care as long as he requests nothing shameful or disgraceful. Because he loves her, he will not hurt her or allow any body to cause her any harm. He cares about her more than she cares about herself. He has requested to change the place of their meeting protect her reputation. This proves his true concern about her, when she meets next time she will tell him that she loves and trusts him, and she is ready to go with him in his car, spend with him the time which satisfies him anywhere he likes as long as they will not be too late and as long as no body will see them. She spend the night sleepless expect a few minutes before sunrise. She waited in tension and anxiety feeling too tired and fatigued until it was time for school. She left the house but she did not find him waiting her, by the end of the school day she harried to the park but she found the park was empty. However, she stayed waiting hoping he will appear at any moment but he did not come. She heard the Muezzin calling for afternoon pray from the microphone of a near mosque. She was forced to go home her heart filled with fear. Will he never come again? Will he leave her forever? Does he desert her, she will get made if she does not see him again, Oh! If only she knows where to find him. She knows little about him. She must have known everything about him.

salma has no friend or companion to tell her that the person whom she thinking that he loves, cares about her, the only one she believed that he will pull her out of the abyss of her sadness, is nothing more than a big imposter and that his absence is deliberate, and he know well that she will goes with him to any place because he know to what extent he deceived her that he is honorable and sincere man, and that he Will finally discard her and throw Her in the street without caring about her tears after destroying her and her honor as he did with many women and girls before her.

How many girls have lost their dearest thing they, have lost their virginity . their honor. How many women thought that he loved them? But they discovered too late, that he only adores himself, his lust and pleasures. How many women went with him in the middle of the darkness at night and the result was the destruction of their future and lived after that in eternal darkness.

17

A week had passed since Salma last saw Osman. When she goes out every day and not finds him she gets more sad and desperate. She was so younger, delicate and sensitive. She has no experience in life. She has nobody to disclose to him what is in her inner self and ask his advice to tell her what to do. Every new day she feels that life is gloomier than the past day. She felt miserable and depressed to the extent that she refrained from food. She reproached herself severely for what she did unjustifiably to Osman. On Saturday morning she sat in the classroom. So absent – minded and distracted unable to understand what her teachers was saying the same as all last week. The school day came to an end. She felt no desire to go home. Last day her stepmother went too far in annoying and ridiculing her. She felt she can no long bear more sarcasm. The only place she can go to was her grandparent's house but she has no money to pay for the bus fare. When else can she go? She found a compelling desire to go to the park as she used to go with Osman. When she arrived she went directly towards their familiar tree at the far corner of the park. She had the fare intended to spend some time to quieter herself then leave but when she was approaching, she found Osman sitting at the same place with his back to the wooden bench, his head in touch with big stem of the tree, his hands on his lap holding a withered red rose and his sight fixed in something unseen. She could not believe her eyes. Her pulse accelerated as if her heart is going to leap out of ribs. She became breathless, and confused for a long while. She could not move . . . sweat followed profuse on her face and handless. She was very Tension; ten of questions come to her mind. Is he still angry? Won't he speak to her? Must she leave at once to keep her dignity? Dose not he want to see her again or did he come to this place for the same purpose which brought her? However, despite these questions, which attacked her mind like a thunderstorm and despite her fear and hesitation, she found herself walking towards him slowly, shyly and timidly until she stopped a few meters from him. She extended a great effort to control herself, and then she greeted him in a low, intermittent and trembling voice. Osman raised his head and looked at her. She saw in the brightness of his eyes, sadness questioning and astonishment as if he sees her for the first time. The artificial he drew on his face multiplied her perplexity and fear. She casted down her look.

Osman had been waiting for Salma in his car near the school. He knew she will be at the apex of sadness and despair after a week of his absence. He was dead sure that he will be able to make her go with him in the car. He was not planning to go far but when he saw her walking towards the park, he changed his plane within seconds. His tremendous mind started to work of quickly and perfectly. He must precede her and sit in the wooden bench waiting for her, and pretend he does not know she is coming. He exchanged her greeting in a manner that suggested he was not expecting her then he turned his face away from her to perplex her more and drive her to think that he is angry and has no desire to meet her. When he felt she reached the maximum limit of fear, anxiousness and disturbance he knows he succeeded to communicate his massage to her. He became sure she was emotionally affected, but he was afraid if he remained ignoring her like this, her instinctive shyness may drive her to leave the park. Therefore, he whispered injuring in a sad voice:

- "Won't you sit?"

She did not believe he is talking to her and inviting her to sit. She sat for a long while and asked timidly:

- "Are you still angry? "

He side without looking at her:

- "No I am not angry, anyone has the right to accept what suits him and reject what does not suit him but what makes me feel painful

84

is that I discovered after all what was been happened between us, you fear me and have no confidence in me .

His words scared her and the word (was) diffused terror in her heart his allusion that he may abandon her for ever affected her deeply that she hastened to say " No, no I trust you . . . I swear by god I trust you fully . . . please do not be angry with me . . . you don't know what had happened to me all last week . . . to prove that I trust you, I am ready to go with you anywhere, and now, but please don't be angry with me".

A hidden smile of victory was about to emerge on his lips when he saying calmly:

- "I don't care wither you go with me or not, What concerns me is that you cast away your doubts and be sure I am not intending to infect any harm on you simply because you are the most precious thing in my life"

His words dropped in her ears as rain drops fall on barren land. She said impatiently:-

- "I . . . I trust you . . . god knows I trust you . . . and sure about you . . . I apologize for what happened to you by me.

- You don't know what you are for me Salma . . . you are my soul and my eyes with which I see and look to life . . . my life is nothing without you. Believe me I had decided not to come here forever . . . I don't know why I came here on this day and at this hour. Perhaps if we hadn't met today, we might have never met again, for I had decided to go abroad again. Why should I stay here was long as I lost you?

She was shocked and terrified when she heard him mention he is going abroad and asked horrified.

- "Go abroad?!"

Yes, what is the use of staying here if you don't be beside me you don't know yet that hadn't we met and go to know each other; I would have gone abroad long ago. When I came back before some months I was not planning to stay here for long, but when I met you, I decided to stay beside you.

His whispering words touched the nucleus of her heart . . . and her eyes were filled with tears. Silence neighed supreme for several minutes until she interrupted it saying:

- "And now do you still want to go abroad?"

- No, I will never go away as long as you remain in love with me and trust me. If my love is distributed among all population of the world, it will suffice them. I have decided to stay here for ever since I saw you for the first time. Believe me if you leave me, I will leave this country for no return.

She thanked god secretly because he came today to this place at this time and because she met him before he flies abroad.

Salma come home completely changed, no more sadness, pain or fear. As soon as she arrived she started to do the daily routine tasks feeling happy and joyful. Nothing can take the overwhelming happiness she is feeling from the depths of her heart. In the evening she went out to meet Osman at a place agreed upon between her and her lover when they left each other in the afternoon.

She found him waiting for her in the car, she turned her head left and right, she histate while stretching her hand to open the door of the car which she had abstained to ride for a long time. She was a faired and confused like a student about to sit for a final examination.

Osman smiled to assume her and said:

- "We shall go for a short excursion, don't be afraid. The car went fastly far away from her residential quarter and she felt relaxed. Osman stopped the car on the Nile bank at a site he chose especially, and opened the recorded. A quite romantic music came softly from the recorder. Osman dismounted from the car went to a kiosk and brought two cups of fresh orange juice then sat again at his seat. He knew she is perplexed and any wretch less behavior from him will spoil his plans. He restrained his violent desire burning inside him.

He about to arrive to the end of the road. By agreeing to ride the car and come here with him, she crossed the most difficult phase. There will be a few such excursions to achieve his goal if things went as he planned. He keeps his thoughts inside him and as experienced person knowing well what his words does in her heart and how flattery infected in soul of a young girls facing such circumstances, he started his sweet talk about her beauty, and about his infatuated with her pure spirit and sublime soul. He told her about his interest, hopes and aspirations to build their future.

As a young innocent and inexperienced girl she was deeply affected. The moon was bright, there was a gentle breeze and the waves were moving to and fro breaking gently on the bank of the Nile. Salma forgot herself. She was quite absorbed in his honey speech until he stopped talking and reminded her that they will miss her at home. She arrived home very happy and contented. Her confidence in Osman increased. He was more careful than her that she must go home early. He didn't take her to an isolated place. Osman also left her satisfied about his brilliant performance. Moreover, she didn't ask him where were they were going.

She left everything to him. That means she trusts him. His main tasks in the days to come are to make her more assumed and excite in her the feminine desire but cautiously and stir in her the natural instinct.

The same repeated meetings in the park were repeated on the Nile bank but this time he never tried to get close to her. He didn't even touch her hand which he used to hold in his hands and release it whenever he likes. All he did was to bring the juice cups, give her one and look eagerly into her eyes, true and unpretented eagerness unlike his pretension of sadness and pain, although his eagerness was true, hot and violent, yet it emanates from sheer animal desire not from the sentiment of pure love. No dreamy look of a teenage girl can quell or satisfy his torturing desire, and no irritant smile satiates his hunger. His eager look and sweet hypocritic words transport her to another world which she didn't know before they met. She felt assumed and secure with him.

She used to sit unhesitant, as before but quite relaxed looking at his eyes while talking to her unaware of what was going on around them.

When he was certain of her assuredness he came again to hold her hand in his hands, kiss it, and keep his lips stuck to it for a long time. She would as if hypnotized, helpless to withdraw her hand. One day he suggested that they sit in the back seat of the car so as to drink the juice from his hands. As soon as she sat and closed the door, she felt he is moving and getting closed to her until their bodies touched each other. She shrinked and stuck to the door but he put his hand round her neck and placed the juice cup on her lips. She has no way to escape. She swallowed the first dose. He kissed her on her neck. She tried to turn her face away. He kissed her on her cheeks then she felt his hot breath on the side of her neck and left ear. She was petrified. He put the juice cup a side and turned her face to his face, and then his lips touched her lips gently. She becomes breathless as if she had been in a race. Suddenly his mouth covered her mouth. His right hand went on drawing her towards him while his left hand was creeping towards her breast and thighs, for along time she yielded to the desire that burned in her body she try to patient until she couldn't and until she be breathless at that time she gathered the power that it left in her body and pushed him away and opened the door and dismount from the car powerless trying to stand on her feet. He came out of the car, found her trembling and tears in her eyes. He set on the ground pretending repentance and pain waiting for her to be calm. He was expecting her to resist him, dismount from the car but he was not expecting she was going to cry. He felt puzzled and perplexed and sat silent until she became quite. She asked him to take her to home. All along the way he didn't try to speak to her. When the car approached the place he said apologetically:

- "I know you are angry with me... I love you Salma... I couldn't control my emotions... all I did was because I love you... it is true that I go too far but aren't we for each other? Aren't we going to marry soon? What will happen if we take something of what will be our right soon to enjoy ourselves for a short time?"

She opened the door and before she slipped out of the car he added:

- "I will wait for tomorrow, don't be late".

She didn't replay. Her eyes were full of tears. She looked at him silently and left the place without turning head, still a farid. She had wrapped her scary round her lips thinking that people will see the traces of his kissed on her lips. When she was in her room, she stood in front of the mirror looking at her face. It seemed to her that her lips become swollen and wore red.

She pretended to be ill and stayed in bed beseeching God to forgive her. It is true they love each other but they are sinners. They have to wait and be more patient. It is true she consented to ride the car and keep her hand in his but she must not go further than this. There is no way for her but to stop going out with him and sitting together for hours in the car. But he will get angry and travel abroad as he told her before and she lose him forever. She shouldn't stop going with him but should tell him that they must wait until they marry. Therefore, he must not kiss her anymore. She must not allow him to do what he did today and he will not be angry because there is no justification for his anger. He will understand her situation if he loves her truly.

When they went out the second day she was determined not to move to the back seat or allow him to kiss her.

[18]

The car arrived, Salma insisted to sit in the front seat. He seemed upset. She couldn't bear to see him angry. She went to the back seat trying her best to keep at a distance from him as much as possible. He sat without trying to move towards her until she drank her juice then he held her hand. He started his sweet soft words which usually touch her heart too deeply. The electric current crept from her hand to the rest of her body.

The smell of sinful desire spread in the air. He crept towards her until their bodies stuck together. She tried to avoid his lips but he reached her mouth. She tried to push his hand from her breast but the fire which was flaming in her body made her hand relax and fall on her lap. She did the same as last time. She regained her self control and was able to push him away, open the door and dismount from the car to the ground trembling with throbbing emotion and her head was feeling sinful. Her sense of sin had disappeared. She no longer came to ask forgiveness from God or reproach herself. Osman felt she will no longer be able to resist the desire he incited in her. She is about to submit. Time has come to take her to his preferable place. The place where she can't find a door to open and salvage herself from his clutches... the place where he can coerce her to submit to his will. In that place she can never escape from him.

The prey is about to fall in the trap. Nobody can save her. Nobody can extend a helping hand to her.

[19]

Ustaz Jalal opened the door of their house carrying in his right hand a plastic bag containing some tomatoes, cucumber and rocket and a big book as well as his preferable newspaper in his left hand.

When he stepped in the house Sana and Sara jumped from behind the door each one them clinging to one of his arms asking him simultaneously:-

– "Why are you late?"

He heard their movement behind the door but he pretended to be surprised and replied laughing:

– "I was late for thirty minutes because there were few mini buses due to fuel crisis now a day. I had to wait for a long time before a mini bus came to take me".

Sara, his youngest sister stretched her hand and snatched the newspaper from his hand saying.

– "As penalty for your delay, this day you are not allowed to read this newspaper which you love so much".

He said smiling pleasantly:

– "Why should I be punished? I am not responsible for the fuel crisis; also I have no private car to enable me to be punctual".

Sana replay laughing:

- "This is your problem not ours, you have to depend on yourself in solving your problems. What we care about is that you come in time or else you will be penalized whatever might be the reasons of your delay.

He said smiling:

- "This is an unfair judgment".

Sana was about to speak but he said before she could speak:

- Don't be naughty girls, take this bag and run to the kitchen to help mother in preparing dinner, I am about to die from hunger".

Sara at the same age of Salam in the final year of the secondary school. Sana studies at a nearby school. Sara is in the second form of the intermediate stage. They are both at the top of their classes. They both love Ustaz Jalal beyond description. He encompassed them, their older sister Nadia who completed her study and was married in addition to their brother Jabir who is now studying in the faculty of engineering, encompassed them with his love and kind care since their father's death but at the same time not forgetting the firm and resolute whenever need arises. They touched his love, care and concern for them and loved him as they love nobody else and are very careful not annoy or anger him.

Ustaz Jalal insisted to clean the dishes as he always doing after taking dinner with his mother and his two sisters because Jabir comes late from the university. After he wash the dishes he layed in bed to read his newspaper. Sana layed beside him as usual. Sara brought a chair, placed it near his head and started to read the newspaper with him while combing his hair softly with her fingers.

Sara interrupted them several times asking about this and that while they were reading. She suddenly became silent for some time. They knew she was slept. Jalal drew his hand from under her head gently, covered her with the blanket and moved to the other bed to resume reading with Sara. After finishing the newspaper he told Sara he is going to take some rest and asked her do the same. He took little nap and got up on the voice of the Muezzin calling for afternoon prayer. He took a bath and put on his clothes ready to go out. On his way out he found his mother sitting with one of her neighbors' drinking tea. He greeted them and told his mother that he will be late after prayer at the nearby mosque she asked him.

–   "Won't you come back to take tea?"

After coming from the mosque he is used to take tea, converse with his mother and revise with Sana and Sara their lessons but this time he said to his mother:

–   "I have an important appointment I have to go to catch up in time; I will not be too late.

After prayer he headed towards the grand market. Today he knew that Salam's father is working there. When he arrived he went towards the place where drivers of mini buses, which take people to and from the different parts of the city, gather. The place was very crowded. The buzzing of engines was mixed with the voice of drivers whose number exceeds the number of mini buses. A lot of them were unemployed. They come here by habit waiting a chance to work when for instance one of their colleagues becomes ill or die or absent for any reason. They would quarrel on whom for replace the missing one as though their long waiting makes them forgetting even the sorrow for whom that was dead or become ill or leaves his home,

Ustaz Jalal always avoids thinking about the destruction which befell the country and poverty which prevail among most sectors of the community causing them to abandon their constant search for means of livelihood. Many times he finds himself engulfed in grid for the conditions and situations of the people. He asked about Salma's father and found him sitting with a group of his colleagues of different ages and appearance waiting for the turn of his bus. He was wearing an old white garment, a white cap on his head and a black well polished shoe. All his clothes were old but clean contrary to most of those who sit with him. Although his features indicate he is in his late fifties but in fact he is in his late forties. One can't mistake he was from upper class tell down by life from the top to the bottom of the society. When Ustaz

Jalal greeted him he felt his calmness despite his exacting and critical circumstances.

He immediately remembered he saw this face in the newspapers many times in the past. A feeling of sorrow and sadness came over Ustaz Jalal countenance for the misfortune of this noble man when he told him he wants to sit with him alone. Ahmed took him to nearby café, ordered a cup of tea for him and a cup of coffee for himself. They sat talking about public affairs: the market and the rising prices, inflation, fuel crisis, Ustaz Jalal set silent deliberately several times to give him the opportunity to ask him who he is and the purpose of his visit but Ahmed did not ask him anything indicating, by this, his refined intellect and high taste.

Ustaz Jalal found himself obliged to introduce himself:

- "I have the pleasure to introduce myself. I am Ustaz Jalal, deputy headmaster of Madame Asma's school where your daughter Salma studies.

Ustaz Jalal observed anxiousness in his eyes. This is the first time a teacher from his daughter's school visits him at his place of work. But Ustaz Jalal hastened to assure him.

- "You have a magnificent daughter, decent, polite and obedient". He continued to say, when an asking look on his eyes as if saying this why do you have to come if she is as you described".

- "I am sorry to come to meet you here. In fact we sent for you but you didn't come".

Ahmed asked anxiously:

- "Is my daughter all right? And when did you send for me? Nobody asked me to come. If I know that you want to see me, I would have come immediately".

Usatz Jalal said:

- "Your daughter is all right. There is nothing serious, don't worry.

I will explain to you. In our school we have a system or you may call it a custom to offer a financial assistance annually to a certain number of students selected randomly by lot.

The school pays the expenses of transportation in the school bus in addition to the expenses of breakfast on behalf of the families of those who were selected. Your daughter was one of the girls who are selected for this year.

As usual, the school delivers the reward to the guardian of the student to come by himself to pay the bus subscription and deposit in his daughter's account in the school buffet. Due the sensitivity of this matter we are very careful it remains secret between the school and the girls' guardians. The girls are not informed about it".

Ustaz Jalal took the money from his pocket and said:

- "This is the premium of this month, please take it".

Ahmed looked at Ustaz Jalal's stretched hand in surprise. Although he tried to be normal, he felt embarrass. This is the first time in his life to be exposed to such a situation. He used all his life to give not to take. When Ustaz Jalal noticed Ahmed's hesitation he continued encouragingly:

- "This is your daughter's entitlement don't refuse it. It is important for Salma. It will save her time and the stupendous effort she exerts everyday in going to and from the school. More important, it will keep her away from inquisitive eyes and harassment and enable her to give all her time for study. In addition to that, this sum is not from me or anybody else. It is from the school fund which is open to contribution by the girls' guardians. In your capacity as guardian of one of the school girls you are welcome to donate any sum of money, big or small.

At last Ahmed took the money. Ustaz Jalal went on saying:

- "This is the first purpose of my visit but there is another more important issue"

Ahmed kept silent but looked at Ustaz Jalal questioningly. Ustaz Jalal continued his speech:

- "It is obvious that Salma has a problem. She is frequently absent minded, introvert and isolated from her examination results are continuously deteriorating. I think she needs us all to get closer to her and you in the first place. You know better than me that girls in this age are very sensitive. They need constant care and support from those around them. From our part in the school, we shall do our best to help Salma".

To removes Salma's father feeling of embarrassment Ustaz Jalal added:

- "I expect that your one doing your best to give her the required care but Salma is passing through an exceptional stage of her life, and will need more care as she is in her final year. We should all extend a helping hand for her was excellent until the end of the intermediate stage but since she came to Madame Asma's school her record had deteriorated continuously".

A short period of silence passed interrupted by Ustaz Jalal.

- "I am sorry to talk to you so frankly but your daughter possesses, her intellectual faculties which can easily make her succeed in her life. It is unjust to waste such a promising girl".

Ahmed made no comment but asked:

- "Is there anything else I can do?"

- Yes, I want you to accompany Salma tomorrow to the school. Please don't mention anything about my visit. You have to pay the bus subscription in her presence then take her to the buffet to deposit in her account the sum of breakfast for this month, then come to my office to have a little talk. This will raise her morale, make her happy and facilitate our next step".

Ahmed was deeply affected. This was apparent in the tone of his voice. He said:

- "I don't know how to thank you"

Ustaz Jalal pressed his hand saying:

- I have done nothing; I am only doing my duty.

- Even if it is your duty, but I have never seen anybody for long years, dose his duty as keenly as you do.

The two men departed and promised each other to meet tomorrow.

Ustaz Jalal left the market for home on foot. He gave all his money to Salma's father. The school has no such fund as mentioned by Ustaz Jalal. It was a lie fabricated by him to guarantee the success of his endeavors to save Salma. He knew about the relation between Salma and Osman. He saw them that day when he delivered her the envelope and also saw them walking together another day. He investigated about Osman secretly and knew that Salma is in great danger. He attributed the reason of this relation to Salma's loneliness, bad treatment of her stepmother and preoccupation of her advice and admonition in her case with Osman will be futile.

He preferred to keep her away from him by subscription in the school bus. Moreover, the proximity of her father, his love and care may make her less attached to Osman.

He hoped that he attracted salmas father attention and left the effect that want to leave in his soul.

[20]

Before leaving the market Ahmed asked one of his colleagues to take care of the mini bus and replace him until he comes back and walked home because he wanted to be alone and think quietly. The visit of Ustaz Jalal has affected him deeply and touched a sensitive chord in his soul. His speech with him incited a feeling of guilt with regard his daughter. Many questions revolved in his mind. Why did he neglect her for so long? Is Ustaz Jalal who is only her teacher is more careful about Salma and her future than him and more understanding her needs? Actually scarcely know anything about her.

He seldom talks with her; ask about her study or about anything concerning her, how could he know if she is suffering from something or not? He don't know what she eats, how she sleeps, where she goes and when does he comes back. She never complains. He left her affairs to his wife, who from the beginning boycotted against enrolling her at school and said it is better for her to stay at home until she gets married to get rid of her. In the rare instances Ahmed had asked his wife about her she usually says that she is in best condition, and from her part she always does her best to give full time for her to study, she provides her with everything she needs to succeed and proceed forward in school achievement. Is his wife saying the truth? If so, why does Ustaz Jalal say her standard is deteriorating? Why did he try to provide her with the cost of breakfast which he leave everyday to Ikhlas to deliver it to her? Does she deprive her of the money of breakfast? Selma never tells him anything to what Ustaz Jalal alluding when he said he wanted to protect her from harassment? Who is harassing her? Has his daughter grown enough to be harassed by men while he is quite absorbed in his own problems? While he was walking he reiterated the speech of Ustaz Jalal word by word and felt as if a cloud was removed from his eyes. He neglected his daughter. She doesn't deserve this treatment. She is his only daughter from his adorable decedent wife. Had it not been for Ustaz Jalal he might have left her to be lost forever from now on he will follow up all things related to her minor or major. He will give her all the time and care she needs.

He arrived home few minutes before the time of the night prayer, he knocked the closed door and heard the two boys running towards it but he heard the voice of his wife saying to them in an ordering pitch:

– Don't open the door, let her wait".

He knew his wife was referring to Salma, he stood still, he waited for a long time, the blood boiling in his veins, he knocked again, he heard his wife voice shouting resentfully:

– Don't knock the door, we heard, wait until we open it for you".

Then he heard her uttering insulting words and damnation, he kept waiting without saying anything. A long time has passed and the door was still closed. Is his wife deliberately abuses his daughter to this extent while he is quite unaware of what is going on his own house? She was upset when Salma came to live with her. He thought such feeling was transient and will go with time; she objected that Salma should continue in the school with the pretext that his income is not enough to pay for their cost of living in addition to school costs. If she used to give Salma the money he allocated for her breakfast, Ustaz Jalal wouldn't have suggested to paying it Salma. Ustaz Jalal and the rest of the teachers at the school certainly noticed that Salma doesn't eat anything all day. Ustaz Jalal must have invented that story about the school fund. Does Salma endure all this without complaining? Where is she now? Why isn't she at home? Where is she and with whom? Does she go out every day without him? Does his wife mistreat her and drive her to wonder in the streets to avoid her molestation? He was extremely angry; he stands to knock the door violently with both hands shouting for the first time in his life:

- Open the door women"open or I will break it to pieces.

His wife was not expecting him to come at this time, she heard his angry voice and hastened towards the door feeling fear and embarrassment muttering and stammering some incomprehensible words as the result of the unexpected surprise.

- "I didn't know it is you, I thought you are somebody else"
  He asked her angrily:
- Where is Salma? "
  He observed how extremely confused is she, she replied hesitantly:
- "Salma ? " I don't know she is not in the house, I don't know where is she now.

He understood everything, he understood how his wife treats his daughter who lost her mother, and he knew the big mistake he had committed.

The image of Salma's sad countenance came before his eyes painful and suffering although she didn't complain at all, since she came to live with him he didn't make her feel, he is close to her or care about her, he created a barrier between them. She couldn't dare to complain to him because of the huge distance between them. What is wrong with him to be so indifferent about Salma, his beloved child? His toil for livelihood to support his family and the drudgery of work preoccupied all his time that her forgot her and her dear mother who entrusted her to him before she died. Why does he spend most of his time outside the house? Is it because of his work or because of the strange aversion he feels towards the two boys? Where is his daughter now and with whom? Did she go out to look for a kind word? Does she go out to escape from the stiffing atmosphere in the house? Would he lose her? Is it too late to save her? He sat anxiously waiting for her torn up with fears doubts, misgivings and suspicions.

[21]

When Ahmed and Ustaz Jalal said goodbye and each one headed towards his house, Salma was sitting relaxely at the front seat of Osman's car, she was no longer afraid to go with him anywhere without hesitation, her fears and confusion had gone while she was following the sense from the window of the car which was moving in high speed, Osman was sitting beside her quite confident and contented. Today he will see Salma in the extreme moments of her weakness and submission to him. After everything comes to an end, he will see her broken and defeated since this day she will be as a ring in his finger. She will be at his disposal at any time, he will not need to deceive her after getting what he wants from her, he will ask her to come at any time and she will obey. He will enjoy her body for some time and discard her when he becomes board and search for another victim. Then things will be the other way round, she will start to run after him, she will wait long hours to see him. How exhaustive was she?

She had consumed a lot of his effort and time, he glanced at her whispering to himself, she deserves all the time and effort she took from him, she is a marvel of beauty, youth and femininity, she is fascinating, charming and captivating, she deserves to wait for her not for months but for years. She is different from any other girl he knew, but any way his efforts were not without a reward, he will soon reap the fruit. Today she will be helpless, she can't push him away from her as she used to do in the car, ecstasy will over whelm her lips, breast, neck, thighs, bowels and every inch of her youthful body within minutes she will not be able to resist her submission to his will during the past days indicates that she

105

is quite dominated by desire. The blood which gushes in her veins when he touches her will make her melt in his arms within few minutes.

Before they departed the day before, Osman told Salma he is preparing a surprise for her, he will take her to a quite place, and she will be quite pleased with it. When he found no objection from her, he took her to the place where he used to bring his preys; he drove the car directly towards the northern of the town and stopped in front of a big building composed of several floors. It was headquarter of one ministry of the government in the past, the place was old, quite and engulfed in darkness save for a small room on its. Western side adjacent to the main gate. Osman descended from the car and went towards the small room and knocked on the door several times, a tall broad shouldered thin man with a big moustache extending beyond his temples displaying the paradox between it and the thin face in which it grew as if the face is fed from a body and the moustache from another body. The man was wearing an old short garment which displays his boney thin legs and lean wrists, on his head was a red cap which he drew to his forehead in way until it covered his eyebrows, although he was in the middle of his fifties but he seemed as if approaching his seventies, he shook arms with Osman warmly and invited him to come in. the man was the guard of the building since several years, he got acquainted with Osman, when he sneaked one dark night to the back garden of the building with a women but the guard discovered them but Osman told him that he is the son of Isam the high official in the government whom everybody knows, that he will be punished if he didn't let them go. Osman gave him a large sum of money and the guard let them go. Osman came the next day and offered to give the guard a monthly salary to prepare and watch the place whenever he comes with a women, having been in need of the money and having been afraid that Osman might cause his dismissal from work, he accepted the offer, since that day that building became the favorite place for his adventure, he furnished a room in the first floor with the modern imported furniture to lead his debaucheries life freely.

Osman used to use that room when he brings a women or a girl with whom he developed a close relation until it became ordinary for her to enter the building without fear or hesitation, but if it is a new prey he prefers to go to the back garden, he has known from experience that entering the building from the first time is almost impossible although after that it becomes very easy. The majority of women who come for the first do not know exactly what will happened to them expecting to spend a pleasant time and that he won't dare to go too far. They think they can stop him whenever they like at any point without losing any thing, they were not able to grasp that when desire possesses them they become helpless to restrain it, and so they surrender themselves to him to do what he likes to them. They don't know how ferocious he is and to what extent he can go if they tried to repel or resist him. That is why he prefers to satisfy his desire the first time in the darkness of the back garden in the midst of the bushy trees.

Osman halted the car at a short distance from the back gate which lays on a narrow street that separate the back of the building from the back of a nursery which prepare seedlings to be marketed in another place. The width of the street was about two meters and twenty meters long. Because its end is closed various kinds of dirt's had collected and dumped until it was about to be filled with plastic bags, old newspapers and tree leaves.

Osman was sure that everything is all right; he descended from the car and asked Salma to do the same. Salma descended but when she arrived at the gate which Osman opened with the key he took from the guard, she hesitated feeling the desolateness of the place, her heart shrieked, she stood for a long while thinking to go back but also thinking she might anger Osman if she refused to enter.

Osman guessed what is in her mind, and was afraid that her fear may drive her to insist to go back, he addressed her in a pitch of impatience "standing here like this will attract the attention of whom they passed nearer, either you come in or let us go back if you are afraid to enter".

She was afraid he might get angry, at the same time she was afraid of the desolate dark place. At last she decided to enter preferring not to anger him but she asked confusedly "But what if someone saw us inside? " he found on other alternative than lying. This building is our property, no one comes here but me, my father is in business journey outside the country and all the keys are with me even if anybody tried to come in, he will not be able to do so because I will close the gate from inside when we enter.

They stood silent for awhile then she said "We shall not be late, we shall spend a short nice time then go back"

He stepped in leaving the door open; she followed him hesitantly feeling about her way through the dark, narrows and herbaceous pathway, she has two conflicting desires. The first urging her to come in and the other urging her to return, leave the place as soon as possible.

Osman interrupted her thoughts saying "I will shut the gate" he passed by her, his shoulder touched her breast, she shivered.... She heard the iron door bolt closing the gate, and then she felt Osman holding her hand pressing it gently, lifting it to his lips and kissing it....she felt the electric current creeping into her body. Osman was aware of her shivering, he put his left hand in her back, held her left hand, put it in his back and they walked forward, each time his shoulder touches her breast, she feels more desire to enter inside the building and that faint sound inside her urging her to go back, is getting fainter, the place became darker and more shrubby. She halted and whispered "I am scared".

This is the first time for her to go to such a desolate place. It's natural to be scared. Osman's experience taught him how to act in such situations...the only way to make her forget her fear and confusion is to enflame her desire, he turned his head and said quietly: "let us sit here a little" time is passing quickly.

They sat close to each other an old wooden bench, he held her hand playing with her fingers while talking about his love for her and their future until she quiescence, then he held her hand in his hands again, lifted it to his lips and kissed it, then he rubbed his lips with her arm. She didn't move, then he kissed her left cheek, put his hand around her neck, he drew her gently towards him, she was not startled or turned her face away as she in the past, she felt his hot breath on her cheek and left ear and sneaking to her chin and neck... her outer garment fell from her head. He held its fore edge and dropped it behind her back. It dropped on her shoulder and reached the upper part of her body. He wanted to liberate her from the outer garment completely; he stood in front of her, held her hands and drew her to him until she stood up. The outer garment slipped and fell on the ground under her feet, he embraced her tightly, she felt his chest sticking to her breast and his strong arms nearly break her ribs, his legs stuck to her tights, when he started to press her tights with his legs she felt hell burning her, she become dizzy and nearly and nearly collapsed. When he held her and made her sit on the ground and sat beside her while she was shaking and started to kiss her with his trained lips on the most sensitive part of her body, she stretched her legs and leaned back ward with the palms of her hands to the ground behind her back stretched his hand to untie the buttons of her blouse, the faint inner voice came again to warn her and order her to stand up but his warm hand touched her virgin, naked breast, she was extremely excited, she became helpless unable to do anything to protect her honor from the imminent danger, she tried to remain sitting with her legs still stretched, she was no longer able to resist, she collapsed stretching on her back to the ground on the dry herbs. He stretched on her without releasing her breast from his lips.

The most exulting moment in his life is that moment at which he touches a female breast with his lips especially if that female is a virgin like Salma, not only because the breast of a women is her greatest point of weakness, but also because he has an ardent passion with that place, a passion which possess and control him as the drug controls the addict. Sometimes he falls prey to fits which make him like a mad person if doesn't find a women's breast to lick it with his lips. When such fits attack him, he will discharge his lust in any women available to him.

When he was adolescent, he raped the girl who was working with the family as servant, molested the daughter of their neighbor and tore off her clothes but his mother came in time to save the poor girl from her savage son, he even tried to abuse his uncle's daughter who is only nine years old.

Whenever he sees a women his eyes follow her breast unconsciously, his criterion for a women's beauty is the compactness of her breast, his infatuation with that part increases when his lips shift from one breast to the other. This makes him feel like a butterfly moving from one flower to the other and makes the women under him as if she is racing in a marathon which exhausts and dissipates her energy and makes her body shout with lust. His lips moved to Salma's belly and thighs, her petty-coat slipped down, she felt his kisses on her naked body, she became weaker and more helpless.

While she is in a semi trance, she heard him trying feverishly to untie buttons of his trouser …the inner voice echoed faintly inside her, but she quite helpless to respond to it. The feverish desire has possessed her body and deafened her ears; she was only waiting impatiently to extinguish the burning fire in every atom of her body.

But suddenly they heard a firm voice calling: "who is there? Who is there? She came to herself in one go. Osman jumped as if bitten by a scorpion, he saw a ghost of a man moving among the trees towards them, he was very frightened, he ran towards the back gate leaving Salma behind trying to warp her naked body with her outer garment running after him colliding now and then with the long branches stumbling from time to time on the rough ground controlled by fright, she didn't know how she was able to put on some of her clothes and get out. Osman had preceded her, opened the gate and left it open.

When she stepped out of the place, he has already switched the car engine and the lights, he intended to escape and leave her alone. She thought for a moment to run in the opposite direction but the light of the man's torch was following her, she ran very quickly towards the car, opened the car door and threw herself into it just before it leaves the place, at last they were safe. Osman turned to her saying:

–   I don't know who is this man, I don't know how and where he came from, where that ugly dog Mahjoub? And why did he allow this man to come here? When I came back tomorrow I will give him a lesson he will never forget all his life, he spoilt every thing"

Salma said nothing, she put her face on her knees and started to weep silently her body trembling and her heart filled with fear.

Osman didn't know that after he left Mahjoub the guard yesterday, somebody came and told him that his daughter is very ill and was taken to the hospital, he humidly brought one of his friends to replace him, and he was so confused that he forgot to tell his friends about Osman and the girl with him.

The guard's daughter had committed a adultery and was pregnant after being beguiled by one of the youth of the village, she was afraid to be discovered.

Her mother took her to the midwife in the neighboring village to abort her. During the operation she blooded a lot of blood, when her condition worsened the midwife decided to take her to the heath center at the nearly town but she died after half an hour in the health center.

The police arrested the midwife and sent to the girl's family who sent a relative to tell her father that his daughter is very ill. Mahmoud didn't know anything about Osman and his relation with his friend Mahjoub whom he replaced.

He has no idea about the agreement of his friend with Osman, therefore, when he heard low voices coming from the direction of the back garden, he ignored them thinking that he was only imagining things because this is the first time for him to spend the night alone in such a desolate place. But the voices became clearer, he tried to persuade himself that it might be a stray cat trying to climb to bird nests on the top of trees, he was afraid to enter the deserted garden. But suddenly he heard groaning and moaning voice; he dropped his ears to distinguish the voice more clearly and walked slowly towards the garden. When he approached the trees and removed their branches to see what is happening and why this person is moaning, he was frightened to see what seem to be two persons, one mounting the other, he was stunned. He thought one of them was trying to kill the other, therefore, he started to shout, who is there? Who is there?

He saw Osman standing and running very fast when he heard the voice. Mahmoud ran quickly to Mahjoub room to look for the torch and bring some weapon to defend himself if need arises, this took a long time that why Salma found the opportunity to run away before being detected and caught by him.

When he came back, casted the light and searched in the garden, Salma was close to the back gate.

He saw her and understood everything; he was very enraged and ran after her swearing and damning her, when he passed the small gate on the backstreet, the wheels of the car were already moving.

When the car was getting close to the place where Salma should leave for home, she asked him to stop the car before reaching her usual place. He was surprised and said:

–   But we are still a little away from the place"?

Salma said: "please stop here"
Osman stopped the car, she opened the door but before she walks away he said:

– We shall meet tomorrow, we shall go to another place"

The car left the place; she went quickly without saying anything trying to control the tears which were flowing down to her cheeks, thousands of thoughts, fears and questions revolving in her mind.

[22]

Time passed slowly while Ahmed was crossing the courtyard of the house to and fro and then he stretches his head over the outer wall, kneel down to look from the hole of the outer door, sit in the old iron chair or enter Salma's room which he never used to enter except when there are guests in the house to look at her ragged bed and small cupboard...one question buzzing in his head making him boil from anger, fear, anxiety about his daughter ....where is she now and with whom?. It seemed to him that a whole age had passed when hearing low knocks on the door. He hurried to open it; before Salma came home he was determined to know where has she been, with whom? Why did she go out? And from where did she come? But when she arrived, he saw the trace of tears on her pretty eyes and heard her soft voice whispering in surprise: "father?"When he saw fear and horror on her face when she saw him, he suppressed all his questions. His rage was replaced by pity and passionate emotion, he left her to go to her room without any question, he knew that the matter is bigger than he thought and this increased his repentance and self reproach, he lied in bed sleepless, turning from side to side.

As for Salma, who was stunned by the unexpected surprise of her father opening the door, she hurried towards her room and dropped herself on bed very scared, fear bridled her tongue, and blood was nearly frozen in her veins, obsessions attacked her fiercely, her fears grew bigger and bigger thinking: did her father know about her love affair with Osman? Why did he come earlier today? Why has he been looking at her angrily and questioning when he opens the door? And that man who chased her when she was running, has he seen and identified her or was he screened by the darkness to see her well? Will he tell the police and make scandal? Didn't Osman tell her he will not expose her to danger? Didn't he say the building is father property and nobody except him will enter it? How did that man enter then? Was Osman lying to her as he did yesterday? What could have happened to her if that man didn't come and what will become of her if he caught her? Why does Osman focus on her body and breast? What was he planning to do to her when she responded to his demand and went with him yesterday to that place? What was he intending to do after her resistance weakened and she became quite helpless? Wasn't he going to stop or rob her dearest thing she has? Was that the real objective of his relation with her? Does Osman love her truly? No, he doesn't love her, he only wanted her body. Yes that is his real purpose she feels and knows that, why doesn't resist her need for him? Why is she so weak towards him? She doesn't know. All she knows, yesterday he was about to break her virginity and convent her from girlhood to womanhood, she is not certain if she can do without him, does she bear all this love for him? Why is she attached to him in this strange way? Did she submit to him so as not lose him? Now it is after mid night, she heard somebody walking slowly towards her bed. She was afraid and remained waiting and gazing in the darkness. It was her father, she closed her eyes very horrified but she felt his hand drawing the blanket to cover her, then she felt his warm lips kissing her cheek tendency, he thought she was a stamp that tender kiss on her cheeks since years, she tried to control herself but she suddenly burst crying, her father, who was about to step out of the door of the room came back and embraced her, his tears flowing down his cheek feeling as if a taught hand is pressing his heart cruelly.

It was sun rise, it is time to go to school, Salma rose from bed to wash herself she heard her father talking to one of the boys, she waited for him to leave the room, she did not want to meet him, she is still afraid that he might have known what had happened last night with Osman. Time was passing quickly, she was forced to leave the room, she found the courtyard empty, and she went to the path, washed, then returned to the room, put on her school uniform and stopped to tie her scarf around her hair without combing her hair hoping not to be seen by anybody when she is leaving home, but when she heard her father's voice calling her name she left the room, her heart trembling with extreme fear, she found him sitting in one of the old iron chairs, in front of him a table with the tea tray and a number of empty cups in it, the two boys were sitting drinking their morning tea, she sat silently on the only vacant chair, she felt assured when her father poured out the tea and gave it to her hand to hand, she took a sip looking at him stealthily asking herself why he started, since yesterday to care, suddenly, about her and why he over looked asking where she had been yesterday. Surely he doesn't know where she has been or else he wouldn't treat her with kindness and affection yesterday and just now, but shall he know? And what if he knows and what will be his attitude towards her? Would he have embraced her as he did last night? Would he have talked to her and give her the tea by his own hand as he did just now? How could she look in to his eyes if he knew about her relation with Osman? She felt very shameful about herself. She didn't know how she drank her tea, she stood up to leave the house but he also stood and walk besides her saying:

– I will accompany you to school today"

She didn't dare to ask why he wants to go with her to school, fear and horror came back to her again, she was afraid he discovered what happened yesterday in the back garden, her father opened the door.

She saw Osman waiting for her to come out of the house, she was very frightened, and the blood was frozen in her veins. She beseeched God secretly that her father will not notice and Osman wouldn't do something that may attract the attention of her father, she extended a great effort not to look in his direction her father noticed her confusion and the looks of Osman following her attracted his attention.

He deliberately looked into Osman's eyes directly, but Osman turned away his face, her father remembered at once the allusion of Ustaz Jalal when he said "the bus will keep her away from inquisitive eyes and harassment .

They arrived to the end of the street and turned to the street leading to the school, he said: "Go on your way, I will catch up with you later on".

She was surprised why he decided to return. She walked towards the school with many questions in her mind. Her father's early return home yesterday was very strange and what is stranger was that he didn't ask her where she had been.

Why did he come so early yesterday? Why didn't he ask her where she had been and why did she come so late? Why did he come stealthily to kiss her on her cheek? Why should he go to school with her today? Why did he return and why did say he will catch up with her later on? Do they know, at school about her affair with Osman and sent to her father to tell him? Somebody must have discovered what is going on between her and Osman, they must have known what happened between them yesterday, her father must have returned to Osman, what a scandal, what sham, what disgrace, she thought she shouldn't go to school and should escape to any place, however, she preferred to wait. If her expectations came to be true she must escape from the country as a whole, how can she look to her father and to people around her with this stigma smearing her honor and reputation?

Her father returned towards the street post light and saw Osman slipping quickly to another street when he saw him, he couldn't catch up with him, therefore, he preferred to ask Omer who, in few minutes told him everything about Osman and added that Osman comes every day to wait for Salma, he also said he saw Osman many times walking after her.

Ahmed didn't see Osman before but heard casual talk about his father one or two times, he doesn't bother to know about him since he is not used to follows up the news of other people. He said to himself "After destroying my future one of their spoilt boys wants to do the same with my daughter, rob her honor and kill her innocence". He looked towards the light post full of anger, haltered and rancor, he continued saying to himself "this time I will not keep waiting, I will defend and protect my daughter with all my power, I will do everything to keep her away and save from their evil designs, I will teach that spoilt boy a lesson he will never forget. he return home, took a big knife, hid it under clothes, then went back towards Madam Asma's school.

[23]

Ustaz Jalal greeted Ahamed, Salm's father, warmly when he came to see him after the first lecture, he invited him to a cup of tea. Ahamed said:

"I have come to you without mentioning anything to Salma about your visit to me. I haven't told her about what we had agreed upon because I want you to tell me the whole truth, I thought about our conversation yesterday and I want you to be frank with me to enable me to deal with the situation as appropriate as possible. Is there something specific I should know? Is my daughter in danger? Has she a problem I can still solve or is it too late?

Ustaz Jalal told him be assured saying:

– First I don't think that the matter is as dangerous as you may imagine. Second the available time is quite adequate if we made the suitable effort until Salma regains her self confidence. After that it will be easy to improve her school achievement to the maximum level. As I have told you yesterday you have a distinguished daughter, polite, decent and very intelligent, all she needs is to be close to her. She needs special care as any girl in her age, I was informed that she had lost her mother since she was a little child, this multiplies her felling of loneliness and makes her ready to be affected with all that happened in her life and more needy for sympathy, kindness and love, if she doesn't find these things in those around her, she will look them else where".

Ustaz Jalal wanted who to push Ahmed to the maximum degree

er care a father could give to his daughter without increase his anxiety about her, he added:

- I think your daughter lives in a huge emotional vacuum, there might be somebody who might exploit her weakness and need force her to neglect her study, also she might perhaps doesn't find the appropriate atmosphere and the sufficient time for study and school achievement, we are only required to give her more care, prepare a conducive atmosphere, occupy her leisure time in memorization of her lessons and leave no chance for her to be alone, therefore, you must be present with her as long as possible, this will make her feel that you love her and care about her. Also you have to revise her lessons with her day by day or even hour by hour, as for her affairs at school leave that to me I will take care of her in cooperation with Ustaza Samia, if you did what I told you to do, we will achieve our goal soon.

Ahmed murmured emotionally:
"you could be sure I will do all you want.. Once more I don't know how to thank you"
Ustaz Jalal said jokingly: My reward is that Salma regains her former standard and obtain a distinguished result in the final examinations.
I will call her after you go to tell her you have come here and payed the bus fare and deposited a sum of money at the school buffet to be at her disposal, I will take this opportunity to offer my assistance, do not forget to drop at the buffet and the employee responsible for bus subscriptions.
Once more Ahmed murmured feeling great gratitude for Ustaz Jalal.
"I can't express my feelings we are all in need of individuals like you to make life more pleasant... individuals who do not submit to despair and never stop doing good actions for the welfare of their fellow human beings whatever the cost may be ...individuals who fight for the sake of truth whatever could happen to them"
Them Ahmed left Ustaz Jalal his tear about to skip from his eyes.
Salma sat in her class worried, tensioned and restless hundreds of questions revolving in her mind. Did they discover what was going on between her and Osman? Did they call her father for this purpose?

118

Will they expel her from school? In the jumble of the question the bell rang announcing the end of the first lecture of which she understood nothing. The hubbub which usually follow the teacher multiplied her annoyance, thank God the class became quite by the arrival of the teacher of the second lecture.

Salma was still submerged in her endless questions, therefore, she didn't notice uncle Karbous when he entered and delivered a piece of paper to the teacher. Suddenly she heard the teacher saying loudly "Salma Ahmed Salim"she felt as if someone struck her on the face, she started as if a bucket of cold water was poured on her head, she looked around, all eyes are fixed on her, and uncle Karbous standing beside the teacher who called her name again impatiently.

She replied in a confused voice "yes, yes"

The deputy headmaster wants you in his office hurry up, be quick.

She felt dizzy as if the earth is revolving around her, she stood up from her chair dragging her legs behind uncle Karbous towards the deputy headmaster's office feeling at every steps that she is going to collapse, no doubt they knew about her story with Osman. Nobody will forgive her, it is better for her to die than to live stigmatizes with shame and disgrace among people, she didn't know who she arrived at the office of the deputy headmaster, and how she entered and stood with her head bowed to the ground.

"sit down Salma" Ustaz Jalal said with calm voice, she sat in a chair feeling that if he didn't invite her to sit at this moment she would have collapsed.

"your father had been here a few minutes ago " her face grew paler, her breath is about to stop and her limbs grew colder,. He added "he came today to bay the subscription of the school bus on your behalf, from now on you can go and come to school by it with your mates, he also Deposited a sum of money at the buffet for you to buy what you need." She was unable to utter a single word. All her thoughts even confined to what happened yesterday in the background. He added in his calm relaxed voice "Would you allow me to ask you if anything bothering you?"

She replied quickly

"No, no, there is nothing bothering me. I am all right".

He said:

"I will be frank with you. You one a mature and wise girl who knows what is right and what is wrong, I want you to forget that I am your teacher I want you to consider me as your father". Then he laughed saying:

"No, no, I don't want to appear old, let us say your older brother. I will be honored to have polite and has good morals and excellent behavior sister like you did you have honor to have a brother like me?"

Salma felt as if the words she was listening to were descending from a heavenly angel unfamiliar to her. His calmness, decent countenance, refined manners and propriety calmed her. His wells selected a sweet words and his sincere voice touched a sensitive chord in her heart. Tears were about to spill from her eyes. Her feeding of guilt over whelmed her. She said in a trembling voice:-

"Of course/ have the honor to be your sister but perhaps a sister like me will not honor you. I am not as you imagine, you don't know me very well. Perhaps if you had really known me, you wouldn't say what you had just said to me. Tears flowed from her eyes. He remained silent until she became calm and said:

"I know you very well Salma I knows you more than you could imagine. That was why I said what I said to you. I know you one of good stock, deserve better than the descriptions I gave you, I know that the circumstances in which you lived affected your character and will continue to affect you if nothing is done to pull you out of them. I don't want to interfere in your private life but I would like to say to you that every one of us may do the right thing and may mistake but we have to learn from mistakes you have strong character and will. You enjoy the best attributes; do not allow the circum stances of your life defeat you. Our life will never be devoid of some difficulties, hard ships and mistakes. You one now in decisive stage, either you allow defeat to be siege you as long as you live, or overcome it and take the opportunity which may not be available to you again Liberate yourself from captivity of difficulties and pairs and convent them to success and excellence. I know that with your instinctive intelligence and good nature you prefer the second option. It is now early for the final examinations. If you concentrate on your study, you will realize your dream your father's dreams, my dream, your teacher's dream and the dream of all who love you. I bet on you. I am confident you will not fail me. What is required of you is to make more effort. If you need anything don't hesitate, my office always open to you at any time, do we agree Salma?"

She couldn't speak, tears were about to flow from her eyes. She nodded her head as a sign of agreement.

"therefore, no more despair, no more time wasting in useless things... you can go now... don't forget to come to me if you need anything".

Salma came to Ustaz Jalal's office scanned, disturbed and confused, came out of it full of hope. She entered broken, shaken and fragmented and strong and full of confidence. She came out another person as if just reborn. At the end of the school day she took the bus with the others girls. For the first time she responded to her mates conversation and Talks and smiled for their joking and share in it. When she descended from the bus, she found her father waiting for her smiling.

He held her hand and walked together while asking her about the details of the school day and her opinion about coming by the school bus.

She told him all that took place during the school day, then asked him:-

"Why did you take the trouble to pay the bus subscription and deposit the money for me at the school buffet? The distance from home and school go and back is not for and I take food when I come back from school. I know your circumstances very well father. I don't want you" to trouble yourself for me.

He felt as if a knife tearing his bowels. How sympathetic and kind she is to endure hunger, heat and oppression of his wife all the past years while he was unaware of what was going on in his own house. He said:

"Don't engage yourself with these trifle things. I apologize for my negligence during the past years. I want you from now on to concentrate on your study, be frank with me, and tell me if you want anything. You are my only hope now. I depend on you very much. I want you to be the best human being in the word not only for yourself but for me as well. Therefore, do your best to succeed and obtain a result that enable you to be admitted to the best faculties in the University. I and you have to be patient to obtain what we hope for Change your school uniform and have a little rest until dinner is ready".

She felt an over whelming happiness for taking dinner with her father for the first time since long years. Her father warned the two boys not annoy her any more. His wife found she had to pretend to treat Salma finely afraid of his anger. Since yesterday he refrained from talking to her when he didn't find Salma at home. Therefore, she took Salm's cup of tea and delivered it to her in her room. Restraining her amazement and rancor. Salma thought she is dreaming. She took a little nap after tea. She awoke at the voice of the muzzein calling for the afternoon prayer. She went out for ablution and met her father going out to the mosque. He said to her:

"I am going to pray. After that I will go to work and came back early. I don't want you to go out of the house or else I shall be worried about you:

I don't want you to do anything than memorizing your lessons. And homework. When I come back I will revise your lessons with you. Then he added merrily:-

Beware I don't want you to miss any information or datum.

She replied quietly:

"Yes father" she took his hand and accompanied him to the door.

After prayer she sat to revise her lessons but she soon felt bored. She neglected her lessons for a long time. It is not easy to return to them in one go. She had to become used to them gradually. She remembered it's time for her appointment with Osman:

She put on her clothes and stood before the minor to put the last touches on her appearance. She saw the image of her father saying to her "Don't go out or otherwise I will be worried about you. She also reiterated the words of Ustaz Jalal "I will be honored to have a sister like you". I bet on you and your success and "I am confident you will not fail me then she remembered Osman's hand playing with her body, undress her, and the voice of the guard shouting who is there and chasing her. Is she really magnificent as Ustaz Jalal said? Is she of sublime manners and noble morals? What shall he do if he knew she used to go out with Osman and knew what they had been doing? What will be say or do if he saw her lying on the ground naked and Osman over her in that desolate dark place? Osman doesn't love her. He is not interested in what will happen to her. If really loved her, he couldn't take her to that deserted place and lie to her that it his father's and no can enter it. If he cared about her, he wouldn't have tried to role her honor. She is sure if she goes with him now, he will insist to take her to another place same as yesterday and demand more assignments and succeed to take what he wants from her. She will not be able to resist him if they are alone. Many times she tried to hinder him from playing with her body but failed. She had always been weak to restrain him so as not to make him angry. He will not stop unless he achieves his goal he will not care to make scandal that will destroy her future. Those who love her are those who care for her interest and welfare, those who are ready to offer anything for the sake of her success and future. Her father needs her. He must have done the impossible to provide her with what she needs. She must do her best to succeed otherwise she will waste all his efforts. She must maintain her honor and her family's honor for if she committed adultery, she will not only destroy herself but her family with her.

She stood for a long time in front of the minor. At last she changed her clothes and went back to her books.

[24]

Ahmed continued to give more time, love, sympathy and kindness to Salma. In the morning he always insists to carry her school bag, walks with her to the door of the bus and wait until the bus moves, then go to work. He comes before noon to receive her when she comes back from school. When he hears the buzzing sound of the bus engine he immediately opens the door, go to the bus door and take the bag before she descends from the bus. After dinner he usually leaves her to take some rest until the afternoon prayer, and then he would go to her room to awake her, carry the tea pot with him and puts it beside her on the table. When she starts memorizing her lessons and makes sure everything is all right he leaves the house again to his work. In the evening he used to revise with her what she memorized. After supper she takes a large cup of milk and goes to sleep. He bought her a new dress, scarf and a pair of shoes. She became more self confident and no longer afraid to mix with her mates. Although the transformation which took place in her father's transaction with her is big and radical, she didn't try to engage herself in searching for its causes. She was satisfied with its results and impact on her life. She was filled with happiness, tranquilly and true paternal love. She will never forget that he used to sneak to her room in the middle of the right to draw the blanket on her body and stamp a tender kiss on her forehead thinking that she is fast asleep. She knew that Ustaz Jalal played a hidden role in all the transformation which took place in her father's relation with her. That is why she feels great sisterly love and respect for him. Home is no longer a detestable place. She even became eager to come to it at noon after the end of the school day. At school Ustaz Jalal follows her progress day by day. When she told him she found difficulty in understanding the past lessons, he requested her teachers to revise them with her in the spare time. Ustaz Jalal allocated some of his spare time to revise Arabic language with her. Arabic language became her favorable subject. Her time became crowded. She preoccupied herself with studying and memorizing her lessons. The reminisce of Osman grew fainter and fainter until finally faded away from her mind as a transient scenery fades away from the window of a fast train. She no longer cares if he is dead or alive. If she sees him by chance she doesn't bother about him. She is no longer in need of his false sentiments. Her outlook to life has totally changed. One day she listened to her mates talking about his disgraceful reputation and thanked God that he saved her from him before it was too late. After several unsuccessful attempts to resume their relation he became desperate and left the street totally to look for a new victim feeling it was the first time for him to be defeated.

Abetment energy was generated into Salma, as well as strange insistence and determination she never knew the like a hungry person who was deprived from food for a long time and suddenly found a table full of all kinds of delicious food. Her standard advanced fastly that her teachers were astonished and became more enthusiastic to help her. If she fell bored from study and memorization of her lessons and felt she has a need for change, she would go to help Ikhlas in household work voluntarily. Her stepmother stopped annoying and harassing her since the day in which her father warned her not to molest Salma or charge her with any work however slight until the end of the final examinations. Salma didn't want to help her stepmother only for changing her routine but also to get closer to her and be friendly to her to improve relations with her. She forgave all the cruel treatment she received from her in the past and tried, with her pure heart, which does not knows malice or hatred to treat her as a daughter treats her mother hoping that Ikhlas will finally respond to her kind treatment and change her attitude towards her but Salma failed to convent her stepmother's hatred and rancor to love and kindness because Ikhlas thought Salma was the direct cause of Ahmed's tough and harsh treatment to her. Since that time when he asked her about where Salma has going, he stopped talking to her except for necessity. What makes her hate Salma more is that she replaced her in shouldering the burden of all household work. Therefore she thought she must get rid of Salma. She thought. The best thing is to solicit help from someone who keeps the secret between him and her only. She thought the only person who could deal with matter safely without her being accused is Sheikh Ali. But how could she find him after all these years. She doesn't know if he is alive or dead. Even if he is alive where is he now? She investigated secretly about him but without success. She didn't know he was arrested by the police after discovering his atrocious deeds and debauchery. He is now in prison for the rest of his life. And he couldn't help himself.

When Ikhlas failed to locate Sheik Ali's place, she decided to depend on herself. She started to give more care for Salma, became friendlier to her and attends for all her needs until Ahmed and Salma though she had really changed and is now trying to compensate Salma for the past cruel treatment. She multiplied her efforts to please Ahmed and Salma. She started to encourage Salma to memorize her lessons and make more effort to obtain excellent results. Salma was happier to see this radical change in her stepmother.

Ikhlas continued to adopt make Ahmed and Salma more confident in her as part of her evil plan to get rid of Salma without being accused of doing that. One thing she persisted on doing daily is to prepare a cup of lemon juice which she insists Salma must drink before going to school.

Examinations were approaching quickly. Salma multiplied her effort that her father became worried about her and the strenuous effort she extents. When the decisive moment came Salma's body grew thin, her complexion became pale-yellow, and her eye- lids were ulcerated. She entered the examination hall the first day. She felt fear controlling her, sweat poured profusely down her face, contradicting eminencies came to her mind at that momement and accumulated as black clouds. She felt as if the examination paper is written in hyrglofic language. She couldn't understand anything she was very terrified. Suddenly Ustaz Jalal appeared. She heard his voice in his last advice to her "At first you may feel frightened in the examination hall; you may think you are not going to understand a single question. Read the questions carefully. You will be more quiet and assured. Repeat reading the questions two or three times before you answer anyone of them". She did as he advised and found everything easy.

The examinations were about to end. The last examination was Arabic language, the day which Ikhlas had waited eagerly to carry out her evil plan. She knew that failure in Arabic language deprives the failing student from the pass mark even if he obtained maximum marks in the other subjects. The lemon juice cup is her means to implement her plan. She knew there is a certain kind of person if a small amount of it is mixed with water or juice and taken by somebody, symptoms similar to the symptoms of malaria would appear on him and will lose consciousness within a short time but the person recovers the next day as if nothing had happened. Because it is difficult to identify this poison Ikhlas will not be accused. On that day Ikhlas woke up early prepared the lemon juice put the poison in it and waited. When the time came, she carried the juice to Salm's room with a wicked smile on her face. Salma was a little worried. She has no desire to eat or drink anything. She is feeding the huge responsibility. Today is the Arabic examination. The subject which will decide the result of the examinations. Besides, it is the subject taught by Ustaz Jalal. She tried to apologize that she has no desire to drink anything but Ikhlas insisted she must drink the juice. Salma asked her to put it on the table until she finishes combing her hair. Ikhlas put the cup and waited to make sure that Salma will drink it to the last drop. But she heard her husband calling her. She quickly went out of the room feeling upset. One of the boys came running to the room. To make Salma upset he took the lemon cup and poured its contents on the ground and ran out of the room. Salma carried the table and put it on the place where the juice was pound and left the room. Ikhlas came to see what happened. When she saw the empty cup she was very pleased and smiled malevolently thinking that Salma had drunk the poisoned juice. She waited anxiously to hear the news of her plot. Ahmed came home at noon. Her wonky and tension increased. She was afraid that she exceeded the permissible quantity of poison and Salma died. She expecting, at anytime, the ambulance carrying Salma or she was kept at the hospital after losing her consciousness. She heard the movement of the bus.

All her body trembled. Ahmed hurried to open the door. She saw Salma safe and sound smiling cheerfully. She felt as if something heavy is pressing her head she couldn't grasp what happened she hastened to her bed and stayed lying in it for the rest of the day. She has no alternative but to wait for the result of the examinations. But what if Salma succeeded? No, she must not succeed, she will not succeed. Even if she succeeds, she will not be admitted to the university she is not that intelligent to compete thousands of students. If Salma succeeded what will she does? She will do anything to get rid of her completely this time. She will increase the quantity of poison. She will not leave her to spoil her life while she enjoys her life.

Examinations ended. Salma was not quite sure about her performance. Sometimes she feels her answers were excellent but other times she feels they were not good. What worries her most is that the efforts of her teacher, particularly Ustaz Jalal may be coasted. The days become empty after being crowded and throbbing with movement and activity. Ikhlas was back to her old customs of harassing and creating problems to Salma. One day her father said to her at dinner when he noticed how she was bored

"What do you think about spending some days with your grandparents"?

She was very pleased. She was in red need for change and for keeping away from Ikhlas and the two boys. She hastened to put her clothes in a small bag in a few moments she stood before her father saying.

"I am now ready, let us go". He said to her smiling jestingly "Wait a little, at least give a few minutes to change my clothes"

She said smilingly:

"I will give you only ten minutes" beware; I will stay with my grandparents the whole holiday.

This was exactly what he wants. He smiled feeling quite relaxed.

Salma was welcomed warmly as usual. She felt at once she is comfort table and at ease. Her grandmother insisted to sit beside her about everything. She told her about her fears and anxiety about the examinations. Her grandmother assured that she will obtain an excellent result.

She said:

You have done your best. Do not engage yourself about it. Forget it now. Do not think at all about it leave it until the time of its announcement comes. You must clean your mind and concentrate with me because I would like to introduce you to very fine and intelligent girl like you.

Salma asked:

"Who is this girl?"

Her grandmother replied:

"One of our old neighbours, engineer Ali, who was an expatriate for years, came back home finally. His daughter, who is in the same age as you, grew to become a beautiful bridegroom. Although they arrived shortly before the examinations, she was admitted to the school of our residential quarter and sat for the examinations. I have told her everything about you. She is eager to see you. I will send for her now you will love her as I do. Once Samira came in Salma felt she likes her when she saw her quiet familiar face. They talked together as if they were old friends. Since that time they never depended. They sleep together one day in Salma's grandparents' house and the next day in Samira's family house.

Salma found a good companion and friend in Samira. She gradually forgot her anxiety about the result. She self that Samira is close to her therefore she told her everything about her school, her mates and teachers. She talked about Ustaz Jalal extensively. While she was talking about him she felt strange sensations towards him not like her feelings towards Osman and of course unlike her feelings towards her father. She missed that kind care, with which he encompasses her, that sound logic and that solemn quiet voice. She longed to see him. Many times had she asked herself what will be her destiny if he did not interfere in her life?

The holiday ended. It is time for announcing the result, the day which all people in every part of the country are waiting for around radios and televisions to watch the press conference held annually by the ministry of education for this purpose. On this day the minister usually casts the light on the result in general, and then announces the first hundred students on the level of the country and the level of the country and that will be the end of the conference. Afterwards each secondary school sends its representative to take the result of his school.

As any other family Salma, her friend Samira, Salma's grandparents and two of their neighbours sat around the television to watch the press conference. Salma was restless and worried.

As the last preparations before the announcement of the result, were going on, Salma hurried to the kitchen with the pretext of preparing tea.

She was very worried. She had to go to the school tomorrow to see her result. She felt she has not sufficient courage to do to that. What will she do? How will she deal with this critical situation? She found herself invoking God to make her succeed (Oh, God, you know I did what I could do, I leave the rest to your providence). Tears flowed from her eyes and covered her face. She heard Samira calling her to hurry up for the names of the first hundred students were about to be announced. She rubbed her tears. Carried the tea tray and went towards the room. Once she entered and before she put the tea tray, she hears the minister with his loud sonorous voice uttering her name.

- "Salma Ahmed Salim- Madame Asma school for girls, the third student on the country level. For a moment she did not grasp what she heard inspite of the rejoicing shouts which came out from those around her. She stood stunned for some seconds as a lifeless statue. When her mind grasped the news, the tea tray fell from her hands and she fell unconscious on the ground beside the tea tray shouts grew louder but this time terrified. The news was beyond her endurance. She is so exhausted to bear such striking news.

[25]

Ahmed left his wife alone at home and went to his parents' home to be present with his daughter when the conference begins to assure her and arrange with her to go together tomorrow To the school to see the result. After Ahmed left the house. Ikhlas prepared some coffee for herself and switched on the television to watch the conference. She listened attentively and smiled when she imagined how her husband will be disappointed when he sees the result of his daughter tomorrow. She started to think about her new plan to get rid of Salma. She convinced herself that Salma will not be able to succeed. Therefore when the minister mentioned Salma's name she felt as if a bullet has pierced her heart. The coffee cup fell from hand at the same moment the tea tray fell from Salma's hands. She felt a sharp pain in her throat and some unknown hands stifling her breath. She stretched hands for a breath of air to inhale but she couldn't breathe. She tried to shout but no voice came out of her mouth. She began to shiver in the old bed like an epileptic and twist like a snake until she fell on the ground. At that moment the two boys came running to the room to ask her something but when they saw her bellowing a slaughtered ox, quite motionless, her limbs desiccated, her tongue stretched out of her mouth and her eyes bulged out, they became frightened, ran shouting and dashed out to the street for help but a rushing car crashed them. People gathered from everywhere. One of Ikhla's neighbours entered the house to see why her neighbor was not present at the site of the traffic accident. She found Ikhlas lying on the ground motionless. She and her sons were taken to the hospital in an ambulance. The younger boy died at once and the older died after two hours. Ikhlas was paralyzed. Only her eyes and tongue could move.

When she knew the bother sons died even her tongue seized to more and remained lying in lead more dead than alive.

Salma didn't know how long had she remained unconscious but she felt hot drops falling on her check. She opened her eyes slowly and saw her father's face looking and smiling at her tenderly and anxiously. She raised her head on the bed. He embraced her joyfully. She looked around and saw all faces smiling at her joyfully she became sure that she was not dreaming and she was able to realize the miracle. It seems to her as if she heard Ustaz Jalal's voice saying to her:

- "I am sure you care going to achieve a dazzling success and obtain what you deserve.

She felt an overwhelming desire to see him at this moment, an irresistible and unrestrained desire. She forgot her usual shyness and said to her father decisively and abruptly.

- "I want to see Ustaz Jalal father... please takes me to him... I would like to be the first person who will communicate to him the news of my success... I want to thank him for all that he did to me".
  Her father said surprised.
- "Just now?"
- Just now, immediately father... I want to see him immediately.

Her father didn't want to spoil her pleasure. They took leave of the others and went out, stopped a taxi.

She asked the driver to speed up. Salma was too anxious but she couldn't know why. She didn't know why she was feeling she is in a race with time as if she is not going to find him. All her thoughts and emotions were concentrated in one thing: to see Ustaz Jalal and see joy in his eyes for her brilliant success in which he had the lion's share. He was the only one who pulled her out of a sea of dankness about to swallow her. But why is she so anxious?

Is it true that she only want to communicate to him the news of her success and thank him? If that is her only motive why is her heart beating like this? And why is body trembling like a small bird in a cold winter night? How could she explain this desperate desire to see him? Does he become to her more than were teacher who extended a helping hand to his student? Why is she thinking about things she shouldn't be thinking about? She must expel these thoughts from her mind at once.

Salma knew the residential quarter in which he lives but she didn't exactly know the location or address of the house. They had to ask the passersby several times until they arrived to it:

She etescended from the taxi hurriedly towards the closed door and knock on it hastily several times. They stood for a while until the door was opened by a girl about fourteen years old wearing a white long-sleeved blouse and a black skirt extending to her feet, her black soft, hair was wrapped like a ball on her head. She beautiful despite the apparent sadness in her large eyes. Ahmed noticed a questioning book in her eyes. He hastened to say:

"My name is Ahmed and this is my daughter Salma, a student in Madame Asma School. We came to see Ustaz Jalal. The girl invited them to come in.

Her voice was Sad. Salma's heart beats accelerated. She entered the house as if drink. The house was small but quiet and comfortable. Ustaz Jalal's mother received them in the saloon. She embraced Salma kindly once she was introduced to her and said sadly:-

- "He was always talking about you and your intelligence. Jalal's mother felt that this girl whom she didn't see before share her sadness for the departure of her son.

She heard Verb (was) and she couldn't control herself. She burst crying bitterly feeling as if she has fallen in a dark hole without depth. He imaging the worst and think bad something happens to him, His mother rubbed her tears saying:

- "If you came a little earlier you would have met him. He leaves to the airport about half an hour ago. His aero plane will take off in about half an hour.

Again she feels a white hand, a good hand pulled her up of that deep dark hole feelings were a mixture of joy, sadness and sorrowful . She said in a trembling voice.

- "you mean he is all right, praise is to Allah, thank God.

- Yes, he is all right but he left to catch up his plane he had decided to go abroad since the end of this school year as he was dismissed from the ministry of education for common good but he post roomed his journey to attend the ministry's press conference. He has been expecting your name to be announced among the first ten students. He insisted to hear it here than in any other country. Tears of joy flowed from his eyes when he heard your name.

Salma shouted painfully:-

- "But Ustaz Jalal must stay… he must not go away… we have to catch up with him at the airport before his plane takes off… we have to do something to persuade him to stay with us. Hadn't it been for him, I wouldn't have succeeded. He helped me to regain myself confidence and stand on my feet again he was saved me. Tens of his students are in need of him to help them as he did with me.

The warmth of her sincere enthusiastic words made his two sisters ask

- "Do you think he will change his mind if we catch up with him at the airport and begged him not to leave?"

- At least we have to try… I must see him … I must talked to him … even if he insists to go abroad."

His mother said:-
"We had tried to dissuade him from leaving the country but he was determined to go. He loves this country more than any other country in the world but he insisted he has no other alternative country. We are all in need of him his sisters don't stop crying since they knew he is determined to travel away." Salma said:-

- "Let us try again… we will lose nothing anyway, allow Sara and Sana to go with me to the airport. Perhaps we might succeed in changing his mind."

They took a taxi hoping to catch up with before it is too late.

The road to the airport was crowded. Salma's tension was increasing. Cars were creeping slowly towards the airport. Salma was impatient. She descended from the taxi and told them she will try to run to the airport before them. She started to run indifferent to the astonished eyes following her. She arrived to the departure hall breathless. The security police was talking to some body. So she took this opportunity to enter easily. She asked about the plane of Ustaz Jalal. She was told by the security officer it has just taken off pointing to it in the air. She watched the plane rising in the space feeling as if her soul is departing her body... The departure hall was crowded with all kinds of people leaving the country. They are running hurried from here to there as if something is chasing them. The plane disappeared in the space. Her payed attention to the people chattering around her:

- "Are you travelling away?
- Yes.
- "Why"?
- "Why! Say why do I stay here, what makes me stay? But since you are asking me let me also ask you why are you going away?"
- "To survive ... To survive... We are almost dying of hunger here"
- "And you why are going away?
- To look for work. All the doors of work are closed here".
- "And you sister why are you going away! To avoid losing my honor, to pre serve my dignity.
- And you brother, why do leave your country?
- To open my mouth and speak, to say what afraid. My tongue got rotten.

Suddenly salma's shoulder touched another woman's shoulder who asked her

- "And you my daughter" why are you travelling?

Salma looked at the women. Her eyes filled with tears, pointing to the sky:

- "I am not travelling but it is he who is travelling:-"
- Who is he who is he young girl?"
- My homeland... It is my homeland that is travelling... it is going away.

[26]

The door of room number five on the ground floor of the people's hospital, where Ikhlas is staying since she was paralyzed, was opened. Salma's face appeared at the door. Ikhla's tears flowed on her cheek as she used to do wherever Salma come to visit her. Salma hastened to rule Ikhlas's tears saying:

- "Didn't you promise to meet me with a smile not with tear, Salma put her hand in her head and continue in her kind and sweet words until she saw her smiling faintly. Salma is now at the beginning of third year, faculty of Arts, department of Arabic language. Which she loves whole heartedly preferring it to any other faculties including medicine engineering and pharmacy. She has chosen this specialization because she is planning to become a teacher like Ustaz Jalal. People had long seized to visit Ikhlas including her husband Ahmed who heard about her disgraceful past and conspiracies. The only person who continued to visit her regularly was Salma. Salma took it to herself that she will love all people like Ustaz Jalal, forgive those who mistreated her, and never bear malice to anybody. The sincere love of Ustaz Jalal and her father had saved her future from being lost and illuminated the rood in front of her. Ikhlas kept weeping in repentance of her dark past. She wished if she could talk for just a couple of hours to apologize for Salma so as to ease her conscience. All people abandoned her with the exception of Salma the only person whom she not only mistreated, but harassed extremely, tortured with hard work, tried to destroy her future and always wished if she disappeared from her life she didn't know

Salma need no apology from her and that her pure heart always forgets the abuse and only remember the good things and the beautiful sweet moments.

(The end)

Bahaa jameel

About the Author

I am very good in describe feeling and analyzing the act of people, I had very strong notice and I hade good imagination

I am avid reader of all sorts of books, novels. Fiction, mystery, politics. E t c.

I was porn in Sudan - Africa, my life is natural, nothing strange except much books, magazines around me. I study in my small town beside the River Nile, I study the college in Khartoum, when I was graduation Iwas comes to Saudi Arabia for work.